the SOCIAL MAZE

JUSTIN ALLEN BERG

Kendall Hunt
publishing company

contents

Part IV: How Do Sociologists Explain Human Similarities and Differences? 103

Part V: Why Do Societies Change?...165

LIST OF BOXES

Box 1: *Using Multiple Perspectives*
Box 2: *Thinking Critically*
Box 3: *Communicating Orally and in Writing*
Box 4: *Solving Problems*
Box 5: *Being Culturally Aware and Building Cultural Capital*
Box 6: *Acclimating to the Workplace*
Box 7: *Recognizing Age*
Box 8: *Avoiding Job Burnout*
Box 9: *Recognizing Stratification*
Box 10: *Valuing Racial and Ethnic Diversity*
Box 11: *Controlling Sexual Harassment*
Box 12: *Searching for a Job*
Box 13: *Office Banter*
Box 14: *Resumes and Cover Letters*

LIST OF SUGGESTED READING

Reading 1: Gladwell, Malcolm. 2008. *Outliers: The Story of Success*. New York: Little, Brown, and Company.

Reading 2: Durkheim, Emile. 1985. "Suicide." Pp. 91–96 in *Readings from Emile Durkheim*, edited by Kenneth Thompson. New York: Routledge.

Reading 3: *Theories of Social Order: A Reader*. 2003. Edited by Michael Hechter and Christine Horne. Stanford, CA: Standard University Press.

Reading 4: Creswell, John W. 2014. *Research Design: Qualitative, Quantitative, and Mixed Methods Approaches*. Thousand Oaks, CA: Sage Publications.

Reading 5: Mears, Ashley. 2010. "Size Zero High-end Ethnic: Cultural Production and the Reproduction of Culture in Fashion Modeling." *Poetics* 38:21-46.

Reading 6: Sanders, Clinton R. 2003. "Actions Speaker Louder than Words: Close Relationships between Humans and Nonhuman Animals." *Symbolic Interaction* 26:405-426.

Reading 7: Shanahan, Michael J., Erik J. Porfeli, Jeylan T. Mortimer, and Lance D. Erickson. 2005. "Subjective Age Identity and the Transition to Adulthood: When Do Adolescents Become Adults?" Pp. 225-255 in *On the Frontier of Adulthood: Theory, Research, and Public Policy*, edited by Richard A Settersten, Jr., Frank K. Furstenberg Jr., and Ruben C. Rumbaut. Chicago, IL: The University of Chicago Press.

preface

After years of studying and teaching sociology, its core perspective and topics have become a part of my life, and I value them greatly. They have helped me better understand myself and my place in society. In writing *The Social Maze: An Introduction to Sociology*, I wanted to share this core perspective and the basic themes of sociology with newcomers to the discipline. My hope is that they will find the information useful in their own lives as well.

I use several techniques to organize this book. I begin with major headings in the form of a question and chapter headings in answer form. At the beginning of each chapter, I offer a bulleted outline of the main concepts and a pedagogical expectation, or something that I anticipate readers will be able to do after reading the chapter. Within each chapter, I inserted questions to assess comprehension and questions that encourage critical thinking. I also use pictures and cartoons to complement the text and stimulate memory recall through visualization. To illustrate how sociological concepts may be applied to real-world situations, I include separate boxes that discuss labor market skills. At the end of each chapter, there is a summary, a list of key terms, suggested reading, and 10 active learning projects that may be undertaken inside and outside of a classroom. The book also includes an appendix that describes the range of jobs that many sociology majors obtain, along with typical salaries. Lastly, there are separate sections for a glossary, a subject index, and references.

I am greatly indebted to many people who made this book possible. Meg Berg encouraged me to write it and spent countless hours reviewing it. The editors at Kendall Hunt Publishing, Jeffrey Huemoeller, Thalia Cutsforth, and Stephanie Aichele, have offered excellent advice and have been a pleasure to work with throughout the whole process. Members of the sociology department at the University of North Dakota have been very supportive. My mentors at Washington State University and Whitman College, although not directly involved, helped me develop a sociological foundation to be able to write an introductory textbook. Finally, I appreciate the students that I am fortunate enough to teach for their inquisitive minds and for their enthusiasm.

PART I

How Do Sociologists Understand Human Behavior?

chapter 1

The Sociological Perspective

Sociologists see life differently. To understand what people do and why they do it and to explain what people think and why they think that way, sociologists do not examine the unique qualities of individuals. Rather, they study the dynamics and consequences of social relationships and social systems. For example, in 2008, Kyla

Brown was an unknown high school student from Massachusetts, but her story was a familiar one: At age 16, she had unprotected sex with her boyfriend and got pregnant. She quickly gained national notoriety when her high school principal accused her of making a pact with several other girls to become teenage mothers (Voss 2008). She denies that there was any pact, saying that she was just unlucky. Other people say that she was sexually promiscuous and someone who wanted attention. Another claim was that she came from a family line of teenage parents. Thus, regardless of the accuracy of the accusations, the majority of the explanations tended to focus on her personal qualities or those of her family and friends.

Sociologists, however, would note that hundreds of thousands of teenagers become pregnant every year (Brindis 2006), suggesting that no personal quality alone can explain the reason why so many unique individuals—who have a variety of characteristics and different family and friends—experience the same outcome. Instead, they would identify the extent to which these young women are living in the same social environment, which consequently influences them to make similar choices. In the United States, the mass media glorifies sexual activity. Thus, it is no surprise that nearly half of all teenagers have sexual intercourse by their 19th birthday (Abma et al. 2010). Sociologists would also point to policies on family education and contraception distribution as explanations for trends in teenage pregnancy (Brindis 2006). In the case of Kyla Brown, sociologists would argue that she lives in a social environment that influenced her behavior and the behavior of her boyfriend.

DEFINING SOCIOLOGY

Sociology is similar to other social science disciplines with respect to its main subject: human life. The following is one definition. **Sociology** is a scientific discipline that describes and explains patterns of human perceptions and behaviors. That is, it examines all the drama of being human—gossip, wars, entertainment, moral values, laws, intimate relationships, criminal activities, religious practices, attitudes, prejudices, and everything in between. The list of topics that sociologists could cover seems limitless.

Since sociology is a scientific discipline, sociologists use the **scientific method** to learn about the affairs of people. Sociologists ask questions, devise hypotheses based on theory to answer the questions, and test the validity of the hypotheses by gathering and analyzing observable data. Some sociologists use quantitative methods, such as random samples and public surveys, to collect their data, while other sociologists use qualitative methods, such as field observations and in-depth interviews. Each type of research uses techniques to systematically gather empirical evidence so that their conclusions can be verified by others.

The knowledge gained through sociological research is valuable for individuals and for societies. On the individual level, people may understand their personal circumstances better when they use a sociological perspective. For instance, persons may get divorced and think that they have failed. The sociological literature, however, indicates that the United States has a particularly high rate of divorce compared to other countries (Furstenberg 1990), suggesting that there is something about the United States that is influencing couples to end their marriages. Large forces, for example, such as changes in the economy and the media, which are beyond the control of the individual, pressure the individual to follow the same predictable pattern as other individuals.

On the societal level, many corporations use the same methods as sociologists to enhance their business models. The retail chain Target made it into the national spotlight because it was using statistics to predict—with upwards of 80 percent accuracy—that certain women were pregnant based on their prior purchases (Duhigg 2012). Then, Target would give them coupons for products that new mothers might want. A father of a teenage girl who was receiving these coupons was enraged, arguing that Target was encouraging his daughter to get pregnant. Later, however, the father apologized by saying that he subsequently learned that his daughter was indeed pregnant. Target knew the behavior of the daughter before the father did.

States and nations may also prepare for the future by examining the sociological literature. Many sociologists study how people react to natural disasters, offering practical information to state and local personnel who have the job of planning for and managing the consequences of these events. Other sociologists who study population dynamics are able to predict what each country's population will look like in the coming decades. China, for example, will have millions more men than women in its population, and many scholars suggest that this type of sex imbalance can lead to an increase in criminal activity and transmittable diseases (South and Trent 2010).

CHECK POINT: What is sociology?

SEEING IS BELIEVING

Sociology is also different from other scientific disciplines with respect to its viewpoint on human behavior. It uses a sociological perspective. In order to gain a better understanding of a sociological perspective, it is worthwhile to spend a little space covering the two other popular perspectives on human behavior: biology and psychology. One metaphor that may help to differentiate biological and psychological perspectives from a sociological perspective is a maze, similar to the one on the cover of this textbook. Imagine

"Sometimes it's good to get a different perspective."

that two individuals are walking through the maze and that only one person eventually makes it to the end while the other person remains stuck inside it. In this case, we might wonder why one succeeded and the other failed—an important difference in individual outcomes. A biological perspective would explain the difference by focusing on a biological distinction between the two individuals. A psychological perspective would point to disparities between the individuals and their immediate environments. But a sociological perspective would concentrate on the maze—the context of the situation. If the maze were structured differently, both individuals could make it to the end, regardless of their biological or psychological strengths or weaknesses. All three perspectives on human behavior are worthwhile. They just pay attention to different things and therefore offer different explanations. For this reason, it is advantageous to be able to recognize the differences in these perspectives on human behavior in order to navigate through the complexities of our own lives.

A Biological Perspective

In order to explain human behavior, a **biological perspective** searches the human body for a cause. For example, media reports often highlight potential genetic differences between people to explain everything from variations in grade-point averages to wealth differences between the upper and the lower classes. Such genetic differences are interesting, and potentially explanatory, and yet they are not the only keys to understanding differences in human behavior. Focusing on the brain is another way to potentially explain behavior differences according to a biological perspective.

The Prefrontal Cortex

The brain is a complex and amazing human organ. Biologists have labeled its different sections based on the functions that each part performs. In particular, within the frontal lobes is the prefrontal cortex. This area of the brain runs the decision-making process. It is activated during times when we think logically and when we struggle to determine what is right and what is wrong or what is beneficial and what is costly. It weighs potential consequences for taking a specific action against potential rewards. In social terms, it helps us stay out of trouble. People are likely to behave differently based on the extent to which their prefrontal cortexes differ (Sakai 2008). We could attribute differences in behavior between two people to differences in their prefrontal cortices. Similarly, these brain differences could account for differing occupational choices, such as becoming a librarian versus an extreme sports adventurer.

Biologists also suggest that the prefrontal cortex does not fully develop until somewhere in our 20s (Brizendine 2011). This may help explain why teenagers are much more likely to engage in risky behaviors than people who are older, and it may offer some explanation as to why people are most likely to commit crimes in their late teens and early 20s. At those early ages, they are just old enough to have some freedom but not old enough for the prefrontal cortex to say, "Whoa, doing that activity isn't worth it." At the same time, biologists argue that this relatively late development of the prefrontal cortex likely helps us survive as a species (Brizendine 2011). At some point, we need to leave the group, or in modern times, the family, to find a mate, but leaving the group is frightening. Since the prefrontal cortex develops after the biological urges to find a mate, young adults are willing to take the risks more so than they might be at older ages. Consequently, we leave our families, find romantic partners, and continue to produce offspring.

Neurons

Even deeper within the brain are billions of neurons. These tiny cells pass information around the brain to allow us to think and move, but importantly the neurons do not actually touch each other. There is a microscopic space in between each neuron. Consequently, the information that runs down the neuron as an electrical signal must transform into a chemical signal. The chemical signal is made up of neurotransmitters. People have different amounts and types of neurotransmitters, which may explain their different moods (Barrett et al. 2007). Numerous pharmaceutical and illegal drugs work in this area of the brain by either adding to an insufficient amount of one type of neurotransmitter or destroying another type of neurotransmitter, and this helps people keep a desired balance in their disposition or a desired feeling of being high.

In the end, biology offers an interesting and powerful perspective on human behavior. Yet, it is important to keep in mind that it focuses specifically on individuals and not groups of people. From a biological perspective, if people do the same things, they must have similar biological characteristics, and, if they do different things, they must have different biological characteristics. So, with respect to the maze metaphor, the biological perspective would pay more attention to the individuals and less attention to the maze itself to explain any differences in human outcomes.

A Psychological Perspective

Psychology provides another important perspective on human behavior. The **psychological perspective** incorporates the environment into its explanation more than biology does, yet it also tends to focus primarily on individual-level differences. Given that psychology is another large and complex field of study, it is prudent to once again narrow the illustration to only a couple of points. Two significant concepts in psychology that relate to explaining human behavior are personality and behavioral conditioning.

The Big Five Personality Traits

For a long time, psychologists have been studying the notion of personality and, over the last few decades, they have identified five personality traits that seem to be fairly stable over time and in different societies: extraversion, agreeableness, conscientiousness, neuroticism, and openness (Heine and Buchtel 2009). Each trait represents a range rather than an either/ or dichotomy. That is, most people are not either extraverted or introverted but rather lie somewhere in between on the scale. Additionally, most people tend to have a little bit of each trait in their personality, although one trait may be more prominent than the other traits, and it is the range of traits that gives a measurable dimension to a person's personality. The overall personality likely solidifies somewhere in the ages between 20 and 30 due to an interaction between the individual's biological makeup and his or her immediate social environment (Digman 1990). After this point in development, personality is thought to remain a part of the individual's core being for life.

© 2013 Cartoonresource. Used under license of Shutterstock, Inc.

"He puts a positive spin on everything."

Here is a brief description of each personality trait. Extraversion refers to the extent to which individuals are outwardly expressive and desire a lot of social companionship. Agreeableness represents the propensity to show compassion and support toward other people. Conscientiousness measures the desire to be self-disciplined and dutiful. Neuroticism reflects the likelihood of experiencing swings of emotion, particularly toward the anxious or depressed side. Finally, openness implies that individuals seek and enjoy variety in most things, such as ideas, experiences, and emotions.

Anecdotally, personality seems to be a very popular explanation of social outcomes. For example, often the justification for two people who end a romantic relationship is that they had incompatible personalities. Additionally, personality is often an explanation for why some people enter certain occupations. It is reasonable to think that someone who becomes a police officer differs in personality from someone who becomes a nurse, especially with respect to the traits of conscientiousness and agreeableness. Or, if a person progresses up the corporate ladder quickly, it is often said that he or she has an ambitious personality. In the end, all of these possibilities and explanations focus on individual differences rather than environmental differences to explain behavioral differences. With respect to the metaphor of the maze, the psychological perspective would suggest that one individual made it through the maze because he or she had a personality suited to succeed in this environment compared to the other individual.

Behavioral Conditioning

One of the founding fathers of the concept of behavioral conditioning was the Russian physiologist and psychologist Ivan Pavlov (Todes 2000). In the late 1800s and early 1900s, Pavlov performed a number of experiments to test the extent to which he could condition animals to have particular reactions; and these experiments in combination with other work led him to win the Nobel Prize in physiology in 1904. Perhaps his most famous experiment was done on dogs and involved food and a bell. In general terms, here is the gist of the experiment: First, he noticed that his dogs salivated at the presence of food. Then, he rang a bell each time he fed them the food. Lastly, he rang the bell without the food and the dogs salivated. The dogs' behaviors were conditioned. They associated the bell with the food and therefore could be manipulated to have a specific physical response.

Since we are animals, too, we fall prey to a similar sequence of events. Such knowledge is not lost on advertisers. This is the basic technique that they use to get us to buy products. It is not by chance that beer commercials portray a seemingly ordinary guy drinking beer and then introduce a number of women who are sexually attracted to him. When men associate the beer with fun, companionship, and sex, they are more likely to experience a positive feeling toward the product and purchase it.

Thus, individuals enact certain behaviors because they have been socially conditioned. With respect to the metaphor of the maze, one individual may have been conditioned to succeed in that environment while the other person was conditioned to fail. Yet, once again, it is important to emphasize that the main focus is still on the individual and not on the maze itself, which is taken for granted and left relatively unexamined. This is where sociology differs importantly from other scientific disciplines.

A SOCIOLOGICAL PERSPECTIVE ⌐══

Sociology uses a unique perspective that pays attention to different things than biology and psychology in order to explain human perceptions and behavior. The **sociological perspective** explains social outcomes by examining the intricacies of a social context—that is, the social environment—in which people reside. The social context may represent a number of situations, including family, school, workplace, and community. The social context may also represent the whole **society**, which refers to the totality of social relations and cultures within an accepted geographic boundary. The social context also includes the ideas of social organization and social patterns. Humans organize themselves in particular ways, and over time engage in recognizable patterns of behavior, which influence subsequent perceptions and behaviors. With respect to the metaphor of the maze, sociologists would be interested in the maze (i.e., the social environment) more than the biology or the psychology of the individuals within the maze. They might ask the following questions: Why is the maze set up this way? How do people engage it? Why and how does it favor some people over other people? What are the immediate and long-term consequences of this type of maze for individuals and for society? How can the maze be changed? Ultimately, the social context (social environment) constrains people to see things in a particular way and to behave in a particular way.

CHECK POINT: What is a society?

The Physical Maze

To further illustrate the social context and how it affects us, it may be worthwhile to begin with a familiar physical maze: city streets. Early in a city's history, groups of people designed, organized, and made the maze of streets, which, on occasion, irritates us because it forces us to do things. We have to take certain roads to be able to go where we want to. We probably take main thoroughfares rather than side streets, but then hit a lot of street lights. Because city planners know the design of the streets and the typical number of cars on the road at specific times of the day, they can time the street lights to keep traffic going in a certain flow. Social organization and social patterns thereby affect our ability to travel around town and make our driving behaviors fairly predictable.

The Social Maze

In many ways, a social maze is similar to a physical maze, because it makes our perceptions and behaviors predictable. In academic terms, a social maze may be thought of as the social environment of a given situation and, to the extent to which sociologists understand the social environment of a given situation, they are able to describe and explain social outcomes. It is similar to the city planners knowing the behaviors of drivers. For example, the movements and emotions of college students are fairly predictable within the university setting. When students go to class, what they feel during finals week, and how they act toward professors compared to office administrators, as well as many other details of campus life, are all predictable to a great extent and not because we know anything about the students' biology or psychology but because we know the maze—that is, the social environment. Moreover, some student outcomes occurred 50 years ago and will likely occur 50 years from now, even though the particular students of course were, are, and will be unique individuals. Since the social environment was, is, and will be similar, the human perceptions and behaviors of so many different people are predictable and understandable.

CHECK POINT: What is the sociological perspective?

The Decision to Commit Suicide

Are all personal decisions influenced by social context? The short answer is: Yes. What about one of the ultimate personal decisions—the choice to end one's life? As unique individuals, there could be a number of distinctive reasons people choose to end their life. In trying to figure out why a friend or family member or someone we know makes such a personal and consequential decision, we might think that we should refer to a psychologist because a psychologist focuses primarily on individuals. At the same time, if we want to understand the larger picture of various important decisions and actions, such as the reasons behind differences in suicide rates at the group level, we could also use a sociological perspective by examining the social context of the situation. That is, each complex behavior has at least two levels to it—individual and group—and different perspectives on human behavior like those of biology, psychology, and sociology may complement each other to come to a full understanding of that complex behavior.

Emile Durkheim and Suicide

In the late 1800s, the French sociologist **Emile Durkheim** used a sociological perspective to explain differences in suicide rates by country (Durkheim 1997). That is, he noticed that some countries had more people in them who committed suicide than other countries. If suicide were purely an individual decision in the sense that the social context had no influence on the person, we would expect to see similar suicide rates in each country, since we are all Homo sapiens at the individual level. Given that there were significant differences in suicide rates by country, Durkheim argued that something about the countries made it more or less likely that the citizens would commit suicide. He chose to study the effects of religion. Some countries at that time were dominated by the Catholic religion while other countries were dominated by the Protestant religion. The empirical evidence suggested that Catholic countries had lower suicide rates than Protestant countries during that time.

t h i n k i n g *critically*

Why might countries with more Catholics have lower suicide rates than countries with more Protestants?

Durkheim set out to explain this pattern of behavior by arguing that some countries have social structures that integrate their citizens into social groups more than do other countries. The religious structure of the Catholic Church requires its adherents to interact with a number of people, a situation which constitutes a social context that influences people to be a part of a group and to have people to talk to regarding difficult experiences. This high level of integration thereby provided a certain degree of social control, such as a network of people to remind other people that suicide would be considered a mortal sin. Simultaneously, it afforded people a means of gaining social support in times of need. The religious structure of the Protestant churches during that period of time required comparatively less interaction with other people. This social context therefore provided less social control and comparatively fewer people to help in times of need. By no means was Durkheim favoring one religion over another. His main point was to show that a difference in religious context helped explain the difference in suicide rates because there was a corresponding distinction in the level of social integration that people experienced in their countries.

Although his book on suicide was originally published in Europe in 1897, and has been subsequently criticized for a variety of reasons, we might wonder if the basic premise holds true today. If we were to examine a map of suicide rates by county in the United States and then also a map of Catholic-dominated counties, we would see that the counties that have more Catholics tend to have lower suicide rates. In these areas, the idea of suicide is likely discussed in different terms based on the different religious networks and proclamations that flow through the population. Ultimately, then, the primary argument here is that even when considering very personal decisions, the social context in which people reside has an influence on them, notwithstanding their unique individual qualities, and this results in observable patterns of behavior over time and in different locations.

JOB SKILLS: Using Multiple Perspectives

You are probably familiar with the phrase, "There's an elephant in the room." It means that there is a topic or problem that is obvious but that nobody is talking about it. Such situations arise in the workplace. One reason why people decline to discuss it is, the solution and consequences may be difficult to handle.

Employees, however, who have the ability to see the elephant or problem from multiple points of view are more likely to find a solution or ways to mitigate the consequences. Part of the problem might be based in biological differences or needs. Other aspects might be psychological. Finally, some of the problem is likely due to the context, the environment, something more sociological. Being able to consider the problem and consequences from a variety of perspectives may lead to some short-term and long-term strategies to solve the problem, or at the very least ways to bring the topic up for discussion.

Here is a scenario: One employee constantly belittles another employee, clearly creating friction in the workplace. What can be done about this situation? Could part of the problem and a potential solution come from biology? Are people getting hungry or need water? Do they have time and space to get up and walk? Providing food and the ability to move around could relieve stress. Is there something psychological occurring? What are the core personalities of the two employees and the boss? Knowing the strengths and weaknesses of each personality may offer solutions for getting along and management techniques. Could the environment be changed? Would rearranging team members help? How would things change as a result of rearranging desks, or adding more light or new equipment? Would instituting quarterly coworker functions and trainings ease interpersonal tensions? Ultimately, solutions that address all three perspectives—biological, psychological, and sociological—would likely make the most difference.

Social Context and Hockey

Social context also influences the likelihood of personal success and failure. When we succeed or fail, or when we see someone else succeed or fail, we often explain the outcome with a description of individual qualities. The person is smart, ambitious, talented, lucky or, conversely, the person is lacking in some or all of the necessary traits. If the explanation is boiled down, it usually falls into the category of a biological perspective or a psychological perspective. Yet, it is reasonable to think that the social environment also plays a role. Malcolm Gladwell (2008) explored this idea in his book *Outliers* by focusing on hockey players. In Canada, it turns out that most professional hockey players are born within the first few months of the year and comparatively few are born within the last few months of the year. This difference presents a conundrum, if we focus solely on individual qualities— because we would expect that people born in December would be just as talented as people born in January. That is, individuals born in both months should have a similar potential to be great hockey players, yet people born in January have a much greater likelihood of realizing that potential.

t h i n k i n g *critically*

Why might some hockey players make it to the elite leagues for reasons other than natural ability?

As Gladwell (2008) explains, the difference comes down to hockey league cutoff dates, which tend to be on January 1 in Canada. To be an elite hockey player, one typically starts playing hockey at a very young age. The cutoff date in combination with biological development advantages one group over another. For example, children who turn 6 years old right after the January 1 cutoff date will be on the same team with children who turn 6 years old in December. Both start the hockey league as 5-year-olds, but the children turning 6 in January have almost a full year of physical development over the group that turns 6 in December. The older children perform better and get comparatively more playing time and coaching, which only makes them even better. By the time both groups of individuals

© 2013 Nikita Chisnikov. Used under license of Shutterstock, Inc.

are playing hockey in high school and college, there is a significant difference in ability and, unsurprisingly, a significant difference in the likelihood of becoming a professional hockey player. What all of this suggests, however, is that if society were to organize its hockey leagues so that the cutoff date were December 1, people born in December would then have a great chance of becoming professional hockey players, or if society switched the cutoff date to February 1, people born in January would not have a very good chance of making it into the elite hockey leagues. Therefore, in addition to any natural or mental advantages, patterns of success and failure also emerge because of social context.

USING A SOCIOLOGICAL IMAGINATION

Being able to see the extent to which a personal outcome is due to individual qualities and when it is due to social environmental structures is valuable. To help people master this ability, sociologist C. Wright Mills (2000) coined the term *sociological imagination* in the late 1950s. The **sociological imagination** has two primary parts to it, what Mills called *personal troubles* and *public issues*. **Personal troubles** represent the unique characteristics of the individual, in particular the characteristics that restrict people from succeeding. **Public issues** refer to problems that are a function of broader social structures in society and which pertain to the specific outcome of interest for the individual.

Mills (2000) offers several examples to illustrate the difference between personal troubles and public issues, including employment and divorce. He says that if a person is unable to find a job in an environment where most other people are employed and the labor market is open, then the personal outcome likely comes down to a personal trouble. The person has deficiencies that constrain him or her from competing successfully. Yet, if a person is unable to find a job in an environment where thousands of people are also looking for work and the labor market is tight, the personal outcome is likely a reflection of a larger public issue, such as unemployment that is due to a change in the economy, outsourcing practices, the replacement of human jobs with advanced technology, or something else that is beyond the control of the individual. With respect to divorce, it may be easy to think that it is a personal trouble. Yet, in a society where almost half of the marriages end in divorce, something beyond the individual must be negatively influencing the marriages. The potential causes are numerous, from the community's views on a lasting marriage to Hollywood's portrayal of romantic relationships, from family tradition to state and federal laws regarding marriage and divorce. Mills continues by saying that a person must also have the ability to not only see the difference between personal troubles and public issues in the present time but over time as well. For example, people who grew up during the Depression in the 1930s had different personal troubles and public issues than people who grew up during the economic boom years after World War II, not because individuals in both time periods were different biologically or psychologically but because the social contexts of their lives were different. The micro problems of our lives may seem personal, but they are influenced by macro events, if viewed historically.

Although Mills (2000) kept the concepts analytically distinct, it is likely that most of our individual outcomes are a result of both personal troubles and public issues. It is just that the majority of people are probably unable to see their personal troubles as outcomes of public issues. Thus, having a sociological imagination—imagining how society influences the individual in all cases—is extremely helpful, because it allows a person to identify the problems and therefore the solutions as being based not only in the individual but in society, too. For example, here is a brief scenario: A person named Maria enters a college math class and ends up earning a D for her final grade. When Maria goes home, she will probably look in the mirror and think to herself that she is just not good in math. She identifies the problem as a personal trouble, and consequently any solution to the problem necessarily would be located in Maria, too. Her success or failure is placed solely on her shoulders, in her mind. Yet, it is naïve to think that the social environment had no effect on Maria while she was growing up and had no effect on her during her time in class.

t h i n k i n g *critically*

Assuming a person named Mary earned a D in her math class, how do we explain this individual outcome using a sociological imagination?

Maria's personal trouble reflects a myriad of public issues. Thousands of students fail math courses every year, and they all do not have the same characteristics as Maria, suggesting that no individual quality can explain why so many different people are experiencing the same outcome. Recognizing that part of the problem originates outside of Maria acknowledges that Maria lives in a society that is interwoven and complex. Federal and state laws determine how much emphasis is placed on learning math while in primary and secondary school. The economy influences parents' ability to spend time with their children on schoolwork. The sports culture affects the amount of time an individual has for studying versus traveling for, playing, and watching sports. The college culture impacts the likelihood of preparing for exams rather than going out with friends. The university structure changes the likelihood of the math course being taught by a graduate student, a new professor, an adjunct professor, or a tenured professor. Since many other forces have already influenced Maria and currently influence Maria, it is worthwhile to identify those other forces in addition to Maria's own responsibility for her grade because they allow her to see that her success and failure are also determined by a larger community. Importantly, then, the solutions are not to be found just on a personal level, but on a societal level, too. Examining the social environment for clues to personal problems offers additional insight into identifying the multitude of causes and potential solutions.

CHECK POINT: What is a sociological imagination?

SUMMARY

Academic scholars and the general public can explain human behavior from a variety of viewpoints, particularly from a biological, a psychological, and a sociological perspective. A biological perspective suggests that differences in human behavior have their origins in biological differences, while a psychological perspective incorporates the ideas of emotional and mental characteristics of the individual in connection with the influences of the immediate social environment to explain individual outcomes. The sociological perspective focuses on differences in the broader social environment to understand why some people behave differently than other people. That is, it identifies variations in the social context of people's lives that pressure people to see and act in a predictable pattern, which highlights the point that unique individuals act in very similar ways regardless of their personal biology and psychology. Sociology, therefore, studies the social context, specifically social relationships and social systems, to understand why humans act certain ways and perceive life the way that they do.

Suggested Reading:

Gladwell, Malcolm. 2008. *Outliers: The Story of Success.* New York: Little, Brown, and Company.

ACTIVE LEARNING PROJECTS

In Class:

1. Look in your wallet or purse and list the contents, or at least five items, on a piece of paper. From a sociological point of view, explain in writing why you have those particular items.
2. In a small group, discuss the following questions: Do people use the social media site Facebook because of something biological, psychological, or sociological? Which perspective plays the biggest role in the behavior? Why?
3. Write about an embarrassing or funny moment in your life and explain why it was embarrassing or funny from a sociological perspective.
4. Calculate the percentage of people in the room who are wearing jeans and explain this fashion choice from the three perspectives.
5. In a small group, search the Internet on a smartphone or tablet for the amount of candy sold during Halloween or pounds of turkey bought during Thanksgiving or ham during Christmastime and discuss why, from the three perspectives.

Out of Class:

1. Watch a reality TV show competition, such as *American Idol, Survivor, Dancing with the Stars,* or *The Bachelor,* and use your sociological imagination to explain why one contestant failed to win.
2. Go to the website learnmyself.com to measure your "Big Five Personality Traits" and explain how this personality test differs from a sociological perspective with respect to understanding who you are and why you are the way you are.
3. Look in your bedroom closet and explain why you have those particular clothes based on a biological, a psychological, and a sociological perspective.
4. Visit a public place, such as a restaurant or coffee shop, and explain why people are acting in certain ways, based on the three perspectives.
5. Write an essay that recounts one of your most memorable experiences, happy or sad, and explain why it happened, based on the three perspectives.

KEY TERMS

Biological perspective

Durkheim, Emile

Personal trouble

Psychological perspective

Public issue

Scientific method

Society

Sociological imagination

Sociological perspective

Sociology

chapter 2

The Emergence of Sociology

The topics of sociology and the sociological perspective are new only in the systematic way that they are examined and used today, not in the sense that people in past ages avoided speculating on the basic reasons of human behavior or focused solely on individual characteristics to explain social outcomes. As far back as recorded history takes us, humans have shown an interest in understanding themselves and their place in the world. The ancient Greeks, such as Plato and Aristotle who lived around 375 BCE, are well known for discussing the drama of human life and offering insightful explanations that incorporated the importance of a social environment. In the 1300s, Muslim historian Ibn Khaldun wrote several books about social conflict and cohesion, among other topics, that theorized the rise and fall of tribes, communities, and civilizations (Fromherz 2011). Then, in the 17th and 18th centuries, the Age of Enlightenment began. During this time period, numerous scholars from several different countries advanced scientific thinking and methodology to comprehend everything from individual morality to political revolutions (Jacob 1998). They were curious about social life. They asked a wide range of questions. They sought to uncover the answers to the questions in a logical and organized manner rather than relying on unverified proclamations of people in authority positions. In many cases, because some of their conclusions did not support the traditional doctrines of the time or coincide with the values and beliefs of their political and religious leaders, they paid the price of their freedom to make these advancements. An important result, however, was that a small minority of people in power began to lose control over the acquisition and distribution of knowledge. The masses now had a means of learning about the complexities of society and a method to test the current explanations regarding the stark differences in social status and wealth among people. They could more easily decide for themselves what was valid and what was not.

THE FOUNDATIONAL CONDITIONS FOR SOCIOLOGY

On the intellectual foundations of the Enlightenment Era, sociology began to take shape as a scientific discipline in the 19th century, and it developed in response to the events of the world at the time. The United States had recently gained independence from Great Britain in 1776 during the Revolutionary War that had included other countries, such as Spain and the Netherlands. A little over a decade later, in 1789, the French revolution began in Europe.

In addition to the political changes, new technologies and capitalistic economies began to evolve in the 1800s, a period in time which was later to be called the Industrial Revolution (Weightman 2010). The **Industrial Revolution** involved a change in the way things were manufactured, grown, processed, and distributed. Mighty machines, such as the cotton gin, the steam engine, and the railroad, replaced human and animal labor. Goods and people could be transported across great distances in comparatively little time. Enormous factories popped up in municipal centers to fashion material items, such as clothes, and to make edibles, such as bread. On the one hand, the family shop struggled to survive because the factories could make the same products more efficiently and cheaply. But on the other hand, a greater number of people could enjoy the products at lower costs. The agricultural producers lost workers, as people moved from the farm to the city to obtain paid employment, but they also benefited from the emergent technologies. As Charles Dickens (1998:1) said in his novel, *A Tale of Two Cities*: "It was the best of times, it was the worst of times, it was the age of wisdom, it was the age of foolishness…we had everything before us, we had nothing before us." The social environment began to have an even more noticeable impact on people's individual outcomes.

Although the opportunities for social and economic mobility were growing and the production of goods and services was changing rapidly, the human price of this advancement was costly for some segments of the population, especially underprivileged workers. Unlike in rural areas, where families and friends often worked the land together, thousands of individuals began to work alongside unfamiliar people in the urban factories. They were not connected to their bosses or coworkers through friendship or family, and the work hours were long and the work environment was dangerous. Many children, even as young as 5 years old, labored 15 hours a day; and men and women were accidentally hurt by the large machines or from doing repetitive physical movements. Many people did not enjoy comfortable, safe homes. The neighborhoods in much of the city's manufacturing sectors were overcrowded and dirty, and rampant with disease and crime—situations that were out of the control of the individual.

Seeing the unembellished conditions of the masses, the intellectuals of the time began to feel compelled to understand the causes and consequences of all of these relatively quick societal changes. They focused their attention directly on the social environments in which people lived and worked in order to find answers to their questions and potential solutions to the social problems. Thus, the social conditions were set for sociology to emerge as a scientific discipline.

Auguste Comte

Numerous scholars contributed to the development of sociology, yet **Auguste Comte**, a French philosopher born in 1798, was one of the first. In the early 1830s, he advanced the notion of **positivism**, which suggests that valid knowledge must come through the testing of observable data rather than moral arguments or thought experiments. He argued that empirical evidence was necessary to support or refute any propositions. After applying this idea to the physical sciences, such as biology and astronomy, he turned his positivistic logic to society with the goal of improving the life chances of the populace. In the late 1830s, he popularized—some say he coined—the term *sociology* in order to carve out a science that systematically examines the problems of society and that can offer meaningful solutions. The idea was that social thinkers would study empirical evidence regarding the connection between the social environment and human behavior. He asserted that knowledge gained in this way would prove more beneficial in designing solutions to all of the social ills he saw around him than moral arguments about worthiness and spirituality.

Comte also argued that over time societies go through several steps in order to acquire knowledge. He called these steps the *Law of Three Stages*. First is the theoretical stage. People gain knowledge through religious leaders and consider the major events and status differences in society to be determined by spiritual beings. Second is the metaphysical stage. In this period, people seek answers from philosophers, who arrange abstract concepts into a logical order, such as Rene Descartes's famous statement: "I think, therefore I am." The third and final stage is the positive stage, which uses scientific principles to uncover the truth of things. For Comte, sociology held the top place in this last stage, because it was a scientific discipline that studied people and the social environment and, therefore, could offer helpful information to everyone else in all other realms of life.

CHECK POINT: Why did sociology become a field of study?

Karl Marx

Although **Karl Marx**, who was born in Germany in 1818, may be thought of as a political economist rather than a sociologist, his life and theories have significantly added to the field of sociology. Like Comte, Marx was also greatly concerned about the state of society and the poor conditions in which people lived and worked during the 19th century. He argued that the social environment, particularly the economy, affected the individual more than people at that time gave it credence. What also sets him apart from other social thinkers was Marx's political activism against the social and economic institutions of the day. For these actions, he was eventually forced out of Germany and then out of France, where he met his collaborator Friedrich Engels, and finally ended up in England. The legacy of political activism has remained strong for many sociologists to this day.

Marx is also well known for writing the *Communist Manifesto* with Engels, wherein they discuss the importance of class and class conflict between the **proletariat** or the workers and the **bourgeois** or the capitalists, who own the means of production. With the term *means of production*, Marx and Engels were referring to the factories and machines that produce the basic goods that people use, such as clothing, food, and other necessities. Whoever owns these factories and machines has power over the people who do the work because they can stop the means of production and thereby terminate the workers' wages and cripple the economy. In a capitalistic system, the owners want

Karl Marx.

to make profits while the workers want to increase wages. Yet, because of the difference in power, they argued, the capitalistic system is structured to exploit the workers and keep their wages low in order to make greater financial gains for the capitalists, forcing the majority of people to live in deleterious conditions while the minority of people enjoy an extravagant lifestyle. This adversarial situation between the owners and the workers is possible because the capitalistic environment supports the notion of private property, according to Marx and Engels. The solution according to Marx and Engles was to unite the workers and start a revolution in order to overthrow capitalism as a mode of production and do away with private property. Then, the workers could own everything together and share the profits equally. In general terms, from their viewpoint, the socioeconomic environment needed to change to help individuals.

For Marx, the economy is the base to everything else because it provides the basic necessities of life. All of the other social institutions, such as the government, religion, and the media, make up what he calls the *Superstructure*, and they rest on the economy. When the economy changes, the other social institutions change. The significant implication of this idea is that the perceptions and behaviors of individuals also change when the economy changes, suggesting that individuals do not have as much control over their minds and actions as they would like to believe. Marx (1979:11-12), therefore, argues that "it is not the consciousness of men that determines their existence, but, on the contrary, their social existence determines their consciousness."

thinking *critically*

What does Marx mean by the statement: "It is not the consciousness of men that determines their existence, but, on the contrary, their social existence determines their consciousness"?

In short, Marx is suggesting that a person's ideology does not determine his or her social context or social environment. Rather, the social context or social environment, which is the economic structure for Marx, is what determines a person's ideology. For example, the U.S. economy switched in the 1970s and 1980s from a manufacturing economy, when it produced a lot of material goods, to a service economy, which functions by providing a variety of services and then importing its needed material goods from other countries. No individual with a specific ideology determined this change in the economy. But the transformation in the economy made a college education more important, because the service industry requires specific intellectual knowledge more than it requires hands-on knowledge. Accordingly, the number of young adults who attend college increased substantially, especially among women and minorities. The result is that their perceptions and behaviors are different than if they had not obtained a college education. Therefore, the economy changes their ideology rather than their ideology changing the economy.

Emile Durkheim

Born in 1858 in France, **Emile Durkheim** also witnessed the struggles of a changing society and wanted to understand it. Many people at the time were worried about the potentially negative effects of individualism, a philosophy that promotes the values of independence and personal goal-seeking over forming groups and conformity. Such a worldview fit nicely with the tenets of capitalism at the time and with the economist Adam Smith's idea that self-interest helps everyone. Smith argued that when individuals compete against other individuals to achieve success and wealth, they produce better items that benefit all people in the end. The question arose as to whether a diverse society of individualistically-minded people could have enough solidarity and cohesion to survive over time.

Durkheim theorized that such a society could maintain a sense of solidarity. In his book *The Division of Labor in Society*, he discusses two types of societal solidarity (Appelrouth and Edles 2008). **Mechanical solidarity** occurs in premodern societies—that is, societies that are based more on an agricultural economy than an industrialized economy. People in these societies have a simple division of labor and most people know how to do the jobs of other people. They engage in similar tasks, learn similar skills, and have similar experiences. Because of this type of division of labor, they also tend to share the same beliefs, values, and identities. Their economy does not require mass groups of laborers who would need to distinguish themselves in order to succeed. Accordingly, the people in this type of society have enough solidarity to survive due to their relative sameness. One modern example is the Amish.

After the Industrial Revolution, however, the division of labor became more complex. People began to work in just one area in the production process and so they did not learn the jobs of other people. Workers were forced to be different from each other. Yet, they still had solidarity. Durkheim called it **organic solidarity**. In a complex division of labor, where many people are doing many different specialized tasks, they need each other to create a finished product. They are interdependent. A popular metaphor for organic solidarity is the body. The brain, the heart, the stomach, and other parts of the body all perform unique functions, yet they also all work together to keep the human organism alive.

Today, the U.S. occupational structure is extremely diverse and interconnected. At the individual level, the farmer needs the grocery store manager, who needs the shopper, who needs the farmer. At an institutional level, the government needs the taxpayer, who needs the business sector, which needs the government. As a world, we are becoming so globalized that what occurs in Asia or the Middle East or Europe affects the United States, and vice versa. One implication of this multifaceted division of labor is that many of our daily interactions with people are shorter and more instrumental— they have a specific purpose—than in premodern societies. Thus, we accomplish a lot, but perhaps we are not as friendly.

In addition to his theoretical and empirical contributions, Durkheim

"I love the sense of teamwork."

© 2014 Cartoonresource. Used under license of Shutterstock, Inc.

made a place for sociology in academia. He developed the first sociology department in Europe in 1895 at the University of Bordeaux. Just as important, he was able to legitimize sociology as a separate and important social science discipline. He argued that sociology was unlike any other discipline, such as biology or psychology, because it had a distinctive way of seeing the social world and analyzing it. He also claimed that there are social facts in society that cannot be reduced down to biology or psychology because they take place beyond the individual, even while they affect the individual. They were, in his words, *sui generis*, which means "of its own kind." Social facts are group-level phenomena, like poverty rates. No biological characteristic or psychological attribute is going to be consistent across everyone who is in poverty, indicating that something beyond the individual is causing so many different people to be poor. Only social facts can explain other social facts. With respect to poverty, an economic recession or a change in the welfare state may be the causal force. Therefore, he asserted that it was important to have a separate, equally funded discipline to study these aspects of social life.

Max Weber

Max Weber was born in Germany in 1864 and, in some ways, flipped sociology on its head. Comte made positivism, the idea that knowledge is best gained from empirical observations, an important value in the discipline of sociology. Through positivism, sociology began to find legitimacy in academia. Durkheim increased this sense of legitimacy with his notion of social facts, which was terminology that was understandable to scholars in the more prestigious fields of the physical sciences because it paralleled their notion of physical laws. Weber, however, said that positivistic sociology that strives to identify social facts is impossible and misguided.

Weber promoted **interpretative sociology**, which seeks to gain **verstehen**—a German word that in the social sciences has come to reflect the notion that researchers should ask individuals to interpret their own behavior in order to understand something about groups of people. As opposed to positivism, which identifies patterns of behavior in humans similar to calculating the patterns of planetary movements in the solar system, interpretative sociology focuses on understanding the meaning behind behavior. For Weber, predicting behavior had very little value if it ignored why the behavior was enacted in the first place. This separates the subject matter of sociology from the subject matter of the physical sciences. When astronomers predict the movement of the planets, pinpointing the forces that lead to these outcomes, they understand the solar system. However, Weber argued that we may predict people's behavior and still not understand why they act that way. As an example, a student may open and close the window blinds every 3 minutes, making his or her actions very predictable, but we still have no idea why the student is engaging in that behavior. Asking the student could reveal his or her own interpretation of the behavior and result in greater understanding of the particular action.

This perspective of sociology relates to the idea of social facts. We may be able to predict marriage rates and still not know why people are getting married. It is necessary to ask people what this behavior means to them. Then, once we identify the meaning behind the behavior we will see that the actions are extremely grounded in culture and societal structures, indicating that there are no universal social facts because cultures and societies are so diverse. Individual and group behavior therefore is too dynamic and too changeable based on different social environments to have stable laws or facts, as in the physical world, as Durkheim implied.

Weber also took issue with Karl Marx's argument that the economy is foundational to all other social institutions. For example, Marx considered religion a part of the superstructure that rested on the economy. If the economy were to change, then the religion would change, too, as seen in the early part of the 20th century when Russia's economy became communistic and religion became less valued. Weber, however, argued that in some cases the opposite occurs. In his book *The Protestant Ethic and the Spirit of Capitalism*, he explained that the Northern European Protestant ethic of work, particularly that of the Calvinist sect, was the precursor to capitalism (Appelrouth and Edles 2008). This work ethic was based on the religious ideals that individual good behavior and wealth were reflections of future salvation in the afterlife. In the process of the religious attendants wanting to secure their salvation, they competed with each other to gain material items and thereby developed a capitalistic economy. Thus, religion was the foundation to the economy in this area rather than vice versa. Once again, Weber demonstrated that universal social facts are an unlikely possibility because the social environment around the world, and even within a society, is so diverse and changeable.

CHECK POINT: How did Auguste Comte, Karl Marx, Emile Durkheim, and Max Weber contribute to the development of sociology?

JOB SKILLS: Thinking Critically

According to a 2006 survey called *Are They Really Ready To Work?*, one of the top skills that employers want to see in new employees is a strong ability to think critically. They said that applicants who exhibit this aptitude have an advantage over others in the hiring process. So, what does it mean to think critically? Here is a definition posted on the website criticalthinking.org:

> Critical thinking is the intellectually disciplined process of actively and skillfully conceptualizing, applying, analyzing...[and]...evaluating information gathered from, or generated by, observation, experience, reasoning, or communication.

Employers want to hire employees who can gather information, analyze its strengths and weaknesses, and apply it in a way that will solve a problem or meet an objective. Here is another list in bullet point form on the criticalthinking.org website:

> A well cultivated critical thinker:
> • Raises vital questions
> • Gathers and assesses relevant information
> • Thinks open-mindedly
> • Communicates effectively

Similar to the historical sociologists, current sociologists and sociology students apply their critical thinking skills to the real-world. Practice thinking critically by imagining the problems in an occupation that interests you (e.g., social workers may worry about the self-esteem of emotionally abused children). *How would you gather, analyze, and communicate information that may solve the problem?*

AMERICAN SOCIOLOGY

Sociological advancements were not only occurring in Europe but in the United States as well. In 1875, William Graham Sumner taught the first sociology course at Yale University and, in 1893, the University of Chicago formed the first sociology department in the United States. In the Chicago area, the sociologist **Jane Addams** co-founded the Hull House in 1889, which is famous for helping immigrants, the poverty-stricken, and women through its social and educational programs. By 1931 Addams would go on to be the first female and only sociologist to date to win the Nobel Peace Prize. In 1895, **W.E.B. DuBois** became the first African American to earn a Ph.D. from Harvard University. Over the next two decades, DuBois wrote numerous works, including the greatly influential book *The Philadelphia Negro* and the collection of essays *The Souls of Black Folk*, bringing the importance of racial boundaries and the consequences of racial inequality to the forefront of sociological thinking. In 1909, he co-founded the civil rights organization, the National Association for the Advancement of Colored People (NAACP), which currently has over 400,000 members and continues to work on the behalf of people of color from all racial and ethnic backgrounds. By 1937, based on the work of George Herbert Mead, **Herbert Blumer** formulated and advanced the innovative theory of *symbolic interactionism*, which has become a staple of sociological thinking. In the latter half of the 20th century, sociology continued to grow rapidly and in numerous directions with a host of different theories and trailblazers. Currently, sociology has its own organization, the American Sociological Association, with over 14,000 members who work in a diverse set of occupations. Sociology is also an academic discipline in most colleges and universities across the United States. Due to their sociological research, sociologists are now invited to counsel a wide variety of organizations and individuals, from local community action networks to the United Nations, and from individual students to a number of U.S. presidents.

SUMMARY

Although sociological thinking has occurred for centuries, sociology as a scientific discipline is relatively new. It emerged in response to the intellectual fervor of the Enlightenment Era and the rapidly changing social environment of the Industrial Revolution during the 19th century. Auguste Comte is typically credited with coining the term *sociology* and also propelled it in a scientific direction through his ideas of positivism. Karl Marx inspired sociologists to be politically active and focus on class conflict. Emile Durkheim added to sociology's theoretical strength with discussions of solidarity and the division of labor and created a place for it in academia as a separate discipline. Max Weber expanded the dimensions of sociology by emphasizing the need to understand the meaning behind behavior and by advancing an interpretative form of sociology in addition to a positivistic kind. In the United States, numerous sociologists also contributed to the development of sociology, including Jane Addams, W.E.B. DuBois, and Herbert Blumer. Currently, sociology has academic departments in most colleges and universities and has scholars who are investigating a multitude of topics and advising a countless number of people and organizations around the world.

Suggested Reading:

Durkheim, Emile. 1985. "Suicide." Pp. 91-96 in *Readings from Emile Durkheim*, edited by Kenneth Thompson. New York: Routledge.

ACTIVE LEARNING PROJECTS

In Class:

1. On a piece of paper make two columns. In one column put the names of the sociologists in this chapter. In the other column put the concepts from this chapter. Without referring to the textbook, draw a line connecting the names with the correct corresponding concepts.
2. Write a letter to the editor of your local newspaper about a community issue using Karl Marx's ideas regarding the bourgeois and the proletariat.
3. Apply interpretative sociology, the idea of discovering how individuals interpret their own behavior, to your personal life by writing a paragraph about doing something that surprised you, saddened you, or made you happy and outline the motivation of the behavior and what the behavior means to you.
4. In a small group, discuss how Max Weber differed in his opinions about sociology from Auguste Comte, Karl Marx, and Emile Durkheim.
5. In a small group, discuss what *sui generis* means and identify some examples in the real world.

Out of Class:

1. Sit through a dinner at a restaurant and identify the interdependent occupations that work together to put the food on your plate, with the goal of illustrating organic solidarity.
2. Find a YouTube.com video that you think illustrates the concept of positivism and explain why you think that it does.
3. Write a short biography of one of the individuals in this chapter and explain why this person is an important figure in sociology.
4. Write an essay that argues why one group (e.g., the Amish) or one country (e.g., Japan) may represent the ideas of mechanical and organic solidarity.
5. Write an essay discussing where the Internet fits into Marx's notions of economic base and superstructure and bourgeois and proletariat.

KEY TERMS

Addams, Jane
American sociology
Blumer, Herbert
Bourgeois
Comte, Auguste
DuBois, W.E.B.
Durkheim, Emile

Economic base
Industrial Revolution
Interpretative sociology
Law of Three Stages
Marx, Karl
Mechanical solidarity
Organic solidarity

Positivism
Proletariat
Sui generis
Verstehen
Weber, Max

PART II

What Theories and Methods Do Sociologists Use?

chapter 3

Social Theory

SOCIOLOGICAL THEORY

The social world is a fascinating place and sociologists want to understand it, as physical scientists seek to understand the natural world. To find answers to their questions and to make sense of the social world, sociologists formulate and test theory. Using the traditional definition, **theory** represents a set of generalized and interconnected statements that explains the reason for an observed pattern (Appelrouth and Edles 2008). This set of statements could be very brief and filled with mathematical formulas, as may be found in the physical sciences. Sociological theories, however, tend to look more like essays. The reason is because unlike in the physical world, the social world does not have laws that are present in every location and over time. For example, sociology has no parallel to the laws of motion, which are stable in every country and time period. When someone drops an apple, it falls to the ground no matter where that person is. As Weber pointed out, to find such consistency in social perceptions and behaviors is extremely unlikely when looking across groups of people in different places and in different generations because the social environments and the cultures are so diverse. Sociologists are also interested not only in predicting behavior but also in understanding the meaning behind the behavior. All of this makes sociological theories appear more like stories in their format than like mathematical equations, yet nonetheless these theories are powerful when used to predict and explain the patterns of human thought and action.

Here is an example of a succinct sociological theory by Herbert Blumer (1958) that explains the reason many Whites express prejudicial attitudes toward racial minorities. Blumer theorized that the process happens in four stages. Majority group members feel superior to members of the minority group. They believe that members of the minority group are significantly different from them. They feel ownership over certain valuable resources. And they believe that members of the minority group want to take the valuable resources. The result is that majority group members develop negative stereotypes, such as

the notion that members of the minority group do not work hard, in order to justify their own privileged position in the social hierarchy and to keep the valuable resources. Thus, Blumer outlined four theoretical statements that are interconnected and end in a logical conclusion that answers the topical question about an observed pattern of social behavior—in this case, racial prejudice.

thinking *critically*

Why else do sociologists use theory?

In addition to explaining a pattern of behavior, theories help us know what questions to ask in order to gain a fuller understanding of the topic. With respect to racial prejudice, we might be tempted to ask the general question: Why are people racially prejudiced? As important as this question is, it fails to lead us in any potentially worthwhile direction to find a distinctive answer. We need a more specific question, and theory can help us define that specific question. For example, from Blumer's theory, we know we could ask: To what extent do majority group members compared to minority group members feel ownership over certain resources? This question is comparatively narrow and focuses on a cause–effect relationship that we can more easily observe and test in the social world.

Another advantage of a theory is that we can find support for it or refute it with empirical evidence. If the empirical evidence falls in line with the hypothesis that was derived from the theory, it then supports the theory's explanation. However, if the empirical evidence fails to follow the predictions of the hypothesis, then the theory's explanation may need to be reworked or it may be false. One hypothesis based on Blumer's theory is that when more racial minorities move into a White-dominated area, Whites will begin to express more racial prejudice because they will fear the loss of significant resources, be it property value or neighborhood safety or something else. This is a testable hypothesis, and scholars have found a lot of empirical evidence for it (Ceobanu and Escandell 2010). The implication of testing the hypothesis is that some theories will be stronger than other theories with respect to explaining the pattern of social behavior. In other words, the strategy of testing hypotheses becomes a measuring stick with which to identify the best theory—that is, the theory that is supported by the most empirical evidence.

Finally, theories help us design worthwhile solutions to social problems (Appelrouth and Edles 2008). To stay with Blumer's theory, since it is well supported by empirical evidence, we know where to focus. We could try a media campaign that shows that Whites and racial minorities are more similar to each other than they are different. We could promote community events that would bring different racial groups into contact with each other to decrease feelings of competition. We could institute educational programs in the schools that examine the processes of racial prejudice and the negative consequences of it for all groups. Without theory to direct us, we might waste our time and money on less effective solutions. This implies that a number of theories exist on a single topic, with some theories being supported by more empirical evidence and offering better solutions than other theories. When various theories are grouped together based on similarities regarding their explanatory statements, they form a **theoretical perspective** or a paradigm, which is a general theoretical framework that presents a unique view of how the social world works. Sociology has three traditional theoretical perspectives: structural functionalism, social conflict, and symbolic interactionism.

JOB SKILLS: Communicating Orally and in Writing

According to the *Job Outlook 2012* survey, conducted by the National Association of Colleges and Employers, employers want new employees to have strong communication skills. In today's work environment, employees must interact with a diverse set of bosses, colleagues, and clients. Building effective oral communication skills will increase the chances of successfully navigating these relationships. For example, as we learned from Durkheim's notion of organic solidarity, which suggests that complex societies have solidarity because different occupational positions rely on each other to function, interaction is likely to be relatively short in duration and have a purpose. This means that people in the workplace in the United States prefer the communication to be clear, quick, and to the point. Practice this skill by answering the following questions that a potential employer might ask in an interview situation:

1. What are your strengths and weaknesses?
2. Why should I hire you over another candidate?
3. What attracted you to this position?
4. What can you offer this company?

STRUCTURAL FUNCTIONALIST PERSPECTIVE

From the **structural functionalist perspective**, **society** is a large social system that has a measurable structure of interdependent parts that function together to maintain survival. One metaphor to aid in visualizing this idea is the desktop computer system. Imagine a monitor, a keyboard, a mouse, and a hard drive. Each part has a separate structure but they are all connected to each other at the same time. Each part has a different function but they all need to work together in order for the computer system to function properly and well. As a whole, it has structures and together it is functional.

The theoretical work of Auguste Comte and Emile Durkheim set the foundation for this perspective. To understand society and the perceptions and behaviors of its individuals, scholars identify the structures of different social institutions and map out the ways in which they all function together. Some social institutions are bigger and more vital to the progress of society, as the hard drive is bigger and more vital than the mouse to the computer system, and some social institutions function better than others during certain periods of time. Yet, they are all predicted to balance each other to reach equilibrium so that the society can advance rather than fall downward toward destruction. A recent example of this equilibrium occurred during and right after the 2007 to 2009 economic recession in the United States. The two principle social institutions during this time were the government and the financial sector. Each social institution was big and important, but the financial sector lost its ability to function well, leading the U.S. society toward collapse. The government, along with its central bank, then stimulated the economy with billions of dollars in aid to struggling businesses and in bank bond purchases to increase capitalization flows and credit availability in order to help stabilize the financial sector and therefore the society. At the individual level, these societal movements had consequences for people, such as spikes in unemployment and divorce rates, disillusionment and anger.

As can be surmised from the example, not all structures function properly. This leads to three important concepts: manifest functions, latent functions, and dysfunctions (Merton 1968). **Manifest functions** refer to the expected and intended outcomes of a part of the system, such as children getting exercise through their participation in the institution of sports. **Latent functions** refer to the unexpected and unintended outcomes of a part of the system. Sometimes these latent functions have positive unintended consequences. Through the institution of sports, for instance, youth get to exercise, learn competitiveness, and enjoy a group activity—which are all manifest functions—but they are also rewarded for their sports participation later in life. Youth who play sports are more likely to earn higher incomes as adults (Stempel 2006), which is a latent function. The sports institution was not designed to help young people earn higher incomes as adults, but because young people carry the skills of competitiveness and teamwork into the labor market they have an advantage over adults who did not play sports during childhood. Other latent functions have negative unintended consequences. Many children injure themselves because they practice too hard or get injured by other players during practice or competitive games. **Dysfunctions** can be either manifest or latent—that is, expected or unexpected—but are always negative for the social system. For example, a manifest dysfunction would occur during finals week of a college semester. It is known that all final exams need to take place in one week, which will unfortunately cause students to experience a great amount of stress. One latent dysfunction is that working students may not be as productive at their place of paid employment during finals week, resulting in negative consequences for the businesses.

t h i n k i n g *critically*

What are some manifest and latent functions that you have experienced in your home and work life?

Criticisms of the Structural Functionalist Perspective

Although the structural functionalist approach has many strengths, it also has weaknesses. Due to its theoretical framework and emphasis on interdependency, it assumes that the social system is a closed system and consequently it has trouble explaining change. That is, it is difficult to explain why any of the social institutions would change, such as increasing or decreasing their functionality over time. If it is due to a change in another part of the system, it is difficult to explain why that part of the system changed in the first place. It becomes circular. Similarly, as this approach highlights interdependence and equilibrium, it minimizes the notion of conflict and any explanations for the emergence of conflict. Lastly, with its assumption of balance, it ultimately supports the status quo as the most functional state, which may not be helpful for a number of less privileged groups.

SOCIAL CONFLICT PERSPECTIVE

The heart of the **social conflict perspective** is Karl Marx's ideas about conflict: a social system offers privileges to one group at the expense of another group and thereby results in a struggle between the two groups for scarce resources. More recently, scholars have extended the groups in conflict from economic groups to status groups, including groups that are defined by race, gender, sexual orientation, age, disabilities, religion, and other status characteristics. This perspective therefore recognizes and emphasizes the existence of diversity in society and assumes that conflict is typical. Different groups within a category, such as heterosexuals and homosexuals, are forced to compete with each other over physical and moral advantages, from tax breaks for married couples to the ability to legally marry and be viewed as morally acceptable. In some cases, it is a zero-sum situation. In a sense, any revenue that is lost due to tax breaks for married couples is limited to a certain extent because gay and lesbian partnerships are forced to pay the taxes. One group saves money from the tax break while the other group pays money because it receives no tax break. In other cases, there are just not enough of the resources for everyone, leading to the struggle over who gets what share. It is no wonder that the debates among Congress members on Capitol Hill are frequently vicious when it comes to designing a federal budget. All groups want a portion of the limited financial wealth.

The groups that enjoy more of the resources have power. A standard conceptualization of **power** is the ability to achieve desired goals despite the opposition of others. The power might be political, economic, religious, or something else, but it suggests that the powerful group members can dictate their own life chances and consequently the life chances of a less privileged group. For example, primary and secondary levels of the education system are currently funded mainly through property taxes. This means that children who live in wealthy neighborhoods attend schools that have comparatively more

"I've told you before, Warner. You're not allowed to spend the entire day complaining until you make partner."

money and typically offer a higher quality education than schools in poorer neighborhoods, suggesting that children who live in poorer areas receive a comparatively lower quality education. Many people have suggested that the state should distribute the property tax revenue equally across school districts, but such legislation never goes very far in the political process because it necessitates limiting the funding of the wealthy schools. The middle-class and upper-class parents of children in the wealthy schools have more political power than the working-class parents due to the political system, which needs money to run smoothly. So, a change toward equality does not occur because the wealthier parents often do not want to give up any resources for their children.

With all of the purported conflict between groups in society, it could seem surprising that society does not implode. One might come to the conclusion that in such a dramatic social environment very little could be accomplished. Structural functionalists might argue that society survives because the different groups need each other—the idea of interdependence— or because the groups have similar values and norms, such as favoring capitalism. Social conflict theorists, however, would reject these ideas. Their theoretical perspective suggests that ultimately groups do not need each other. The members of one group could perform all of the societal functions in the system, from being political representatives to waste managers. It is just that the powerful group prefers the less powerful group to perform the unpleasant work and be exploited for that unpleasant work in the process. Social conflict theorists also argue that not all groups share the same values and norms, but that the powerful groups are able to spread their values and norms across society more easily.

t h i n k i n g *critically*

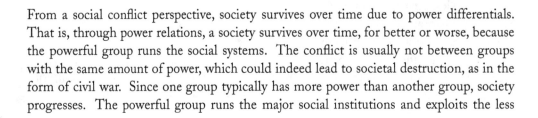

How does a society survive when it is full of conflict between groups?

From a social conflict perspective, society survives over time due to power differentials. That is, through power relations, a society survives over time, for better or worse, because the powerful group runs the social systems. The conflict is usually not between groups with the same amount of power, which could indeed lead to societal destruction, as in the form of civil war. Since one group typically has more power than another group, society progresses. The powerful group runs the major social institutions and exploits the less powerful groups. In the United States, we do not need to look too far to identify that powerful group. In the government, the economy, the military, the religious organizations, the criminal justice system, the education system, the media, and many other places, the positions of authority are filled by middle-to-upper class, White, Protestant, heterosexual males. There may be conflict, but not between equally powerful groups.

Criticisms of the Social Conflict Perspective

The social conflict perspective has its limitations, too. It has trouble explaining consensus and altruism. Given the assumption that groups compete over scare resources, there is little sense in the notion that the privileged group would voluntarily give up any amount of power to the less privileged group. Yet, there is empirical evidence for it. White voters, for example, have supported policies that benefit racial minorities in the areas of employment, housing, and education. Additionally, conflict is assumed to lead to negative outcomes, especially for the less powerful group. However, many positive outcomes emerge through conflict. Competition is a form of conflict but has played a pivotal role in the progress of capitalism, spurring numerous advancements in fields as diverse as the oil industry and the health care industry and leading to a number of political and civil rights for many different minority groups. Lastly, the social conflict perspective ignores the powerful effects of interpersonal interaction and the shared meaning that develops from it, as in the case of grassroots efforts that begin small but have a large societal impact.

SYMBOLIC INTERACTIONIST PERSPECTIVE

Over the first half of the 20th century, American sociologists Charles Horton Cooley, George Herbert Mead, and Herbert Blumer generated and advanced the **symbolic interactionist perspective**. It focuses on micro interactions between people, paying attention to how people use and interpret symbols to create meaning and understanding. The symbols may be tangible, such as a slammed door or the rolling of eyes, or verbal, such as whispers in the ear. Interacting through symbolic communication, people form perceptions about the world and learn to regulate their behaviors when they are alone and in the company of others. From this perspective, society is built on the everyday interactions of individuals. The macro structures such as the economy and the government do not exist outside of micro interactions. Despite large-scale events, such as recessions, people are still free actors with an astounding ability to navigate through and to manipulate the complex social situations in which they live. Even babies, for example, learn to read and communicate with facial expressions in order to achieve a desired outcome.

People construct their social realities in specific social environments through their micro interactions. The **social construction of reality** refers to the notion that people define what is real and what is not real through social interaction within social institutions (Berger and Luckmann 1966), and this perceived reality can have significant and long-lasting effects. For example, many people consider attention deficit hyperactivity disorder (ADHD) to be a result of genetics and not a result of micro interactions—some children are just naturally unable to focus or sit still or listen as well as other children. The solution therefore is to use drugs rather than to change the social environment.

Yet, it is the micro behaviors that professionals endow with meaning when they interact with the children to determine whether a child should be diagnosed with ADHD or not. Todd Elder (2010) suggests that hundreds of thousands of children have been misdiagnosed with ADHD because they are the youngest ones in their kindergarten classes. The outcomes point to the school system as the social context for misdiagnosis. Here is how it works: As a society, we organize ourselves with the socially constructed idea of chronological age and the modern calendar in order to pass people through the education system. Anyone who is 5 years old by a particular date, such as September 1, may enter kindergarten. So, what this means is that some kindergarteners will have just turned 5, say in August, and some kindergarteners will have been 5 for almost a whole year by the cutoff date. That is, they will turn 6 in late September, for example. Consequently, during micro interactions in the classroom where the meaning of behaviors is being interpreted, the younger 5-year-olds will appear comparatively active, less focused, and more distractible than the older 5-year-olds, those who will soon turn 6. The behavior of the younger 5-year-olds therefore is much more likely to be judged as symptoms of ADHD, as they are compared to other 5-year-olds who may be older, because their behavior—in a comparative sense—matches some of the socially constructed criteria of ADHD, which the older 5-year-olds do not exhibit because they are biologically older and better able to control themselves. Consequently, the difference is not ADHD but rather biological development. An unfortunate implication is that many of the younger 5-year-olds who are misdiagnosed with ADHD are subsequently put on various drugs and incorporate the label of having ADHD into their personal identity. They do not actually have ADHD, but, in their socially constructed reality, they do, and this affects their subsequent perceptions and behaviors regarding their strengths and weaknesses and their ability to succeed or fail.

Criticism of the Symbolic Interactionist Perspective

As with other theoretical perspectives, the symbolic interactionist perspective downplays some aspects of social life. With its focus on individuals and the micro sphere, it pays less attention to the effects of large social institutions and group conflict. For instance, the media system spreads culture through society and consequently influences people's perceptions, and therefore symbolic meanings of objects and behaviors, regardless of micro interpersonal interactions. To a certain extent, societal structures create meaning that individuals use rather than vice versa.

CHECK POINT: What are the main points of the three traditional theoretical perspectives in sociology?

SUMMARY

In order to acquire knowledge, sociologists create and test theory, which is a set of interrelated statements that explain the patterns of social phenomena. Theories also help sociologists define new questions to ask about a topic and find effective solutions to social problems. When several similar theories are grouped together, they form a theoretical perspective or paradigm. The three traditional theoretical perspectives in sociology are structural functionalism, social conflict, and symbolic interactionism. Structural functionalism sees society as a social system of interconnected social institutions, which have separate functions to help society survive over time. The social conflict perspective takes for granted that society is socially diverse with respect to having a number of different groups, each struggling against the other for a share of scare resources. Symbolic interactionism focuses on symbolic interpretations that individuals perform during interaction. All three perspectives examine different aspects of society, ask different questions, and come up with different answers, providing a more robust understanding of the reasons behind human perceptions and behaviors.

Suggested Reading:

Theories of Social Order: A Reader. 2003. Edited by Michael Hechter and Christine Horne. Stanford, CA: Standard University Press.

ACTIVE LEARNING PROJECTS

In Class:

1. Picture a college party and brainstorm some of the manifest dysfunctions and latent dysfunctions and some solutions to solve the problems.
2. Think about a main conflict in your life. Write down to what extent you think that it is fundamentally about differences in power by race, class, gender, age, religion, sexual orientation, etc. Propose some solutions.
3. Pair up with another person and write a dialogue between two people, where one person follows structural functionalism and the other person follows social conflict, and the topic is why there is prostitution in society.
4. In a small group, list all of the foods you ate in the last week and discuss why you ate those foods and not other foods, using the three theoretical perspectives.
5. In a small group, think of a number of holidays and discuss what people exchange and why, using the three theoretical perspectives.

Out of Class:

1. Call up a friend or family member and ask him or her to offer an explanation of some topic you find interesting (e.g., why Americans like sports). Identify the statements that could begin to form a theory.
2. Sit in a coffee shop or restaurant and listen for miscommunications or misunderstandings between people. Using the symbolic interactionist perspective, explain why the miscommunication occurred. What symbols were used? What meanings did the symbols hold for the participants? How did each participant interpret the symbolic communication? What symbols did they use to come to an understanding—facial expressions, words, hand gestures, objects, something else?
3. Watch the video *Tough Guise*, and explain why boys and men act the way they do—based on what is in the video—from a structural functional perspective, conflict perspective, and symbolic interactionist perspective, and make a case for which theory you think has the best explanation.
4. Write an essay that describes the last verbal fight you got in and explain why it occurred using the three theoretical perspectives.
5. Watch a TV show and list some of the symbols that make it dramatic or funny or entertaining—that is, identify the things that the TV show uses to create and communicate a world that the audience understands and enjoys.

KEY TERMS

Dysfunction
Latent function
Manifest function
Power
Social conflict perspective

Social construction of reality
Society
Structural functionalist
     perspective

Symbolic interactionist
     perspective
Theoretical perspective
Theory

chapter 4

Quantitative and Qualitative Methods

KEEP IN MIND

- Sociologists acquire knowledge through the use of the scientific method.
- Quantitative methods collect data that are mainly numeric in form and use statistical techniques for analyses to represent a population of people.
- Qualitative methods collect data that are based on observations and use interpretative techniques for analyses to understand the social life of a relatively small group of people.
- Research ethics are a code of behavior that sociologists follow in order to be honest in the research process and protect their subjects' rights and dignities.

BE ABLE TO: Describe the main components of the scientific method and identify the strengths and weaknesses of quantitative and qualitative methodologies for gathering empirical evidence.

SCIENTIFIC METHOD

It is one thing to watch people and offer witty explanations about social situations and another thing to actually go out and investigate the social world. Sociologists want to know whether their theoretical ideas about human perceptions and behavior are supported by empirical evidence. That is, they assume that human actions do not just emerge out of nowhere but happen because something caused them to happen and they assume that they can pinpoint the true cause by gathering and analyzing empirical evidence with the right research tools. In general, they follow the scientific method, which means that they collect data systematically so that other people can verify or refute their findings and conclusions. Below are the five basic components of the **scientific method** (Frankfort-Nachmias and Leon-Guerrero 2011).

1. Ask a question.
2. Define a testable hypothesis based on theory.
3. Collect empirical evidence.
4. Analyze the empirical evidence with scientifically accepted techniques.
5. Evaluate whether the hypothesis is supported by the empirical evidence.

By following this method, any conclusions regarding a certain pattern of behavior are open to other scientists to support, criticize, or change. In this way, sociologists build a body of knowledge that is accepted by the wider community of scientists and from which new research can begin. The research process can be organized into four sequential steps that parallel the steps of the scientific method.

Step 1: Finding a Topic

Sociologists have systematically studied humanity for 200 years, and so a person may wonder whether there are any topics left to examine. Thankfully, since human beings are so complex and because the social environment is constantly changing, a limitless number of topics and questions are still available to investigate. The place to get a sense of what has been studied and what has not been studied is in the research literature. After their academic reports have been accepted by their colleagues, sociologists publish their work for anyone to read. This becomes the body of knowledge on a subject.

Typically, a researcher is curious about some broad area of human behavior and then conducts a review of the literature to narrow down his or her potential research topic. A **literature review** is the process of reading as many studies as possible on a particular area of interest in order to understand the main theories, methodologies, findings, and conclusions. Reviewing the literature helps a person know what questions are being discussed among scholars and what questions still need to be answered.

Sociologists usually pose questions that focus on a causal relationship between two social constructs. A **social construct** is something that humans define, create, produce, or invent through their interactions. They want to know what social construct causes what other social construct and why. For example, in broad terms, a researcher may be interested in knowing what women think about when they look at magazines that only feature fashion models on the covers. The researcher, like Melissa Milkie (1999), may do a literature review and find that a significant relationship exists between the number of magazines viewed and level of self-worth measured. At the same time, what the researcher may realize after conducting a literature review is that no one has studied the relationship between religiosity and self-worth in this scenario. That is, the question becomes: To what extent does religiosity condition women's feelings of self-worth when they view these magazine covers and why? This question reflects a causal relationship between two social constructs—religiosity and self-worth—and it may be based in theories about how religion strengthens or weakens women's self-worth, making them more or less susceptible to media influences, such as the magazine covers. Religiosity and self-worth are both social constructs because scholars have to define what the terms mean in order to measure them in the real world.

Step 2: Deciding on the Research Method to Collect Data

Once the question and the relationship have been selected, sociologists decide on a research method to use in order to collect the data. The literature review and theory help in this decision, because they indicate what has been done before and what would be most productive. The theory may fall in line with macrosociology or microsociology. **Macrosociology** focuses on large societal structures and social systems, while **microsociology** focuses on individual agency and interpersonal interaction. Structural functionalism and social conflict theory are both macrosociology perspectives because they explain behavior as a result of the dynamics of social institutions. In the prior example, one might conclude that women in areas with a lot of religions will feel differently about the magazine covers than women in other areas. Since the social environments are not the same, the women would not be expected to behave in the same ways. Symbolic interactionism, on the other hand, is a microsociology perspective because it examines the interaction between people. Rather than examine group differences in terms of the presence, or lack thereof, of religions, a symbolic interactionist might investigate how women who attend religious organizations create meaning and construct ideas about religion, beauty, media, and self-worth differently than women who do not participate in any religious organizations.

Depending on the theoretical perspective, and what has already been done in the research literature, the sociologist might use either quantitative research methods or qualitative research methods to collect data on the topic. **Quantitative methods** are research techniques that gather empirical evidence that is numeric in form and that can be analyzed with computers. **Qualitative methods** are research techniques that help the scientist gather empirical evidence from field observations and that are typically analyzed thematically.

Step 3a: Using Quantitative Methods to Collect Data

One of the main goals of researchers who use quantitative methods is to test theory. Before the data collection process even begins, sociologists have a theory in mind and want to know whether the theory is supported by empirical evidence. They formulate a hypothesis based on theoretical ideas to directly test with the data. A **hypothesis** is a statement about the potential relationship between two or more social constructs that is a testable answer to the research question. With respect to the example, two possible hypotheses, depending on the theory, may be: (1) After looking at magazine covers, women who attend religious services will express more self-worth than women who do not attend religious services; and (2) After looking at magazine covers, women who attend religious services will express less self-worth than women who do not attend religious services.

The social constructs within the hypotheses are abstract—that is, it is unclear what self-worth means—and so they need to be defined in a way that a researcher can measure them. As a simple metaphor, imagine that someone wants to measure his or her height. Height is an abstract concept, but the person can turn it into something measurable by using a measuring tape. So, height is represented by inches and feet and, in this way, can be applied to everyone equally. In a sense, sociologists use a measuring tape to measure other abstract concepts, such as self-worth and religiosity. They operationalize the social construct and turn it into a variable. A **variable** is a social construct that has a range of measurable values or characteristics and that can influence something else or be influenced by something else. For example, a person's level of self-worth can be measured in the following way: If having self-worth means having confidence in yourself, how much self-worth do you think you have?—(1) A lot; (2) Some; (3) None. The operationalized variable then is typically in the form of a question or statement that requires a response: Are you religious?—(1) Yes; (2) No. In this way, the researchers are able to gather empirical evidence through the operationally defined variables—for example, whether women are religious and their level of self-worth.

Since the hypothesis is a relationship between two variables that typically has a causal direction, sociologists label each variable differently. The causal variable is called the **independent variable**. It is independent because it is not being impacted by anything else. The variable that is affected by something else is the **dependent variable**. It depends on another variable. In the example, the variable for being religious is the independent variable and self-worth is the dependent variable. The researcher wants to know what causes self-worth, and whether being religious causes a certain level of self-worth, according to the hypotheses. In some cases, however, there is no relationship between the two variables. This situation is called a **spurious relationship**, which means that a third variable is causing both of the variables in the relationship. For example, it is possible that education actually causes someone to be religious or not and also causes someone to have a certain level of self-worth. Religion therefore may not actually affect someone's self-worth. The researcher and his or her colleagues have to decide whether the hypothesis represents a valid relationship or a spurious relationship.

One way sociologists determine whether the relationship is valid or not is to control for other variables. A **control variable** is a variable that is held constant when examining the relationship of interest. Here is an example based on agriculture: Imagine two separate fields of corn. One field is green and lush while the other field is brown and dry. What has caused the difference? It could be a difference in soil, irrigation, and sunlight. But a salesman argues that it is a difference in fertilizer. The only way to know whether the fertilizer has an effect is to plant the two fields on the same land and give them the same amount of water and sunlight. Then, use the fertilizer on one field but not on the other field. If the two fields of corn still grow differently, the fertilizer is most likely the cause of the difference because the other factors have been controlled or held constant. With respect to the religion and self-worth example, the researcher would compare women who have the same education level and identify any differences in self-worth and being religious or not. If women who have the same education level differ in their self-worth and also differ in being religious, then it is likely that differences in religiosity resulted in differences of self-worth. Education would not be the causal factor because it was the same for the women.

Surveys

A popular instrument of quantitative methods is the **survey**. It is a series of questions that represent the operational definitions of the variables that the researcher wants to measure. The questions may be on paper for mail surveys, on a computer for telephone interviews, on a portable computer for in-person interviews, or online  as an Internet survey. All of the variables of interest, especially the dependent variable, the independent variable, and the control variables, are put in the survey in the form of questions so that they can measure the social constructs of the hypothesis and eventually provide the empirical evidence to test whether the relationship is valid or not, thereby supporting the theory or not. Some surveys are **cross-sectional**, meaning they reach a diverse selection of people at one point in time, and some surveys are **longitudinal**, meaning that they ask the same people the same questions over a designated period of time.

Surveys have strengths and weaknesses. They are particularly good at measuring people's perceptions, beliefs, values, demographic characteristics, and reported behaviors. Since they do not measure behavior directly, the researchers are forced to assume that people answer the questions truthfully. Surveys also have the advantage of reaching a lot of people in a relatively short amount of time. However, they are not good at observing people's actual behaviors or the interpretations of why people enact those behaviors. They are also weak at capturing any social processes that people go through to come to a perception or to engage in a behavior. Consequently, they might misrepresent people's true feelings and real behaviors.

In some cases, a survey is given to everyone in the population. This survey is called a census. In most cases, however, a survey is given to only a small group of people from the population. This group of people constitutes a sample of the population. Researchers study the characteristics of the sample and then infer their findings to the population. That is, whatever they find in the sample, they suggest it is the same in the population. Importantly, the people in the sample need to be similar to the people in the population with respect to their perceptions and behaviors. In order to gain a sample that adequately represents the population, sociologists use **simple random sampling** techniques. The basic idea is that researchers find a list of everyone in the population, such as a list of telephone numbers, and then generate a set of random numbers to match the desired size of the sample, such as 2,000 people. They attach the randomly generated numbers to the corresponding numbers on the list of people in the population and then encourage those particular individuals to take the survey. This sampling technique is in contrast to asking friends or anyone who is willing to take the survey. Such a group of people would be considered a **convenient sample**. The people in a convenient sample are highly unlikely to represent the rest of the people in the population, because it is improbable that they are a diverse set of individuals who have characteristics that parallel the characteristics of people in the population. A randomly generated sample is much more likely to draw a diverse selection of people from the population. Therefore, samples garnered through simple random sampling rather than convenient sampling offer comparatively valid data for hypothesis testing.

Step 4a: Analyzing the Data and Making Conclusions

Once the data are collected through quantitative methods, such as a survey, sociologists analyze the information. Since the information is numeric, they use a variety of computer programs and statistical techniques. This process may involve calculating simple mathematical formulas, such as the average, as well as organizing information into straightforward graphs and cross-tabulations, or it may involve running advanced computational analytics and complicated statistical models. In either case, the primary goal is to evaluate the probability that the theoretical hypothesis is supported by the data. When quantitative researchers are satisfied that the statistical tests present significant outcomes, they conclude that the empirical evidence favors the particular theory of interest. They consequently argue that they have learned something important about social reality.

Step 3b: Using Qualitative Methods to Collect Data

In contrast to quantitative methods, qualitative methods facilitate an in-depth understanding of the actions and interactions of a relatively small group of people in a particular social setting, which is called the *field*. Sociologists who favor this methodology enter the field for a variety of reasons (Bailey 2007). They may merely want to describe what they see. They may want to evaluate the productivity of some organizational plan. They may want to test some cause-and-effect relationship. They may want to formulate a new theory. Or, they may want to discover individual interpretations of behavior and the social processes in the environment. Yet, in all of these cases, and similar to quantitative methodologists, they are primarily interested in answering some research question or curiosity about humanity.

Observation

The primary technique of qualitative methods is observation. When sociologists are in the field, they can take on a number of different roles to accomplish this task. They can be **complete participants**, where they do whatever the individuals under observation are doing. They can be **complete observers**, where they refrain from doing any of the activities and just watch. They can be **participant observers**, where they take part in some activities but not in others. In all of these cases, sociologists may choose to be overt about their presence by telling the

© 2014 Ron and Joe. Used under license of Shutterstock, Inc

people in the field about the study or they may choose to be covert about their intentions and pretend that they are just another member of the group, especially if the group is engaging in socially sensitive behaviors, anything from race relations to criminal activity.

There are a number of things to observe as well. These include physical spaces, objects, activities and events, timing of the activities and events, actors and their interconnected acts, goals, and feelings. Within each of these categories, other points might be noted, such as smells, speech patterns, and body language. Sociologists attempt to comprehend as much detail as possible about the new social world that they are investigating because it will allow them to make analytical connections at the beginning of the research in order to narrow the focus later on. As sociologists see people in their natural setting, they come to a better understanding of how the social environment—in all of its complexities—actually influences people's perceptions and behaviors.

One potential problem, however, must be recognized and managed. It is called the **Hawthorne effect**, which represents the idea that people change their viewpoints and actions when they believe that someone is watching them or when they believe that they are placed in artificial circumstances. The name arose because, in the early 1900s, certain social scientists studied worker productivity in a factory called Hawthorne Works. They learned that the workers were more productive when observed than otherwise. In some cases, therefore, the researcher may influence the members of the group being observed to act in expected ways, defeating the goal of learning the behaviors of individuals in their natural environments.

Interviews

Another important technique of qualitative research is the interview. Although sociologists may discuss topics with the subjects in the field, an interview is different in the sense that it has the direct goal of eliciting specific information from people for the research project. Conducting productive interviews therefore is a difficult task, especially when the cultural norms and expectations of the subjects are taken into consideration regarding how, what, when, and to whom information may be given.

There are three main types of interviews. The **structured interview** follows an explicit pattern. It is planned beforehand for a specific time and place and the questions are arranged and asked in a precise order. All of

"Before you go for your interview I can touch up your roots."

© 2014 Cartoonresource. Used under license of Shutterstock, Inc.

the participants experience the interview process the same way, with very little participation by the researcher. The advantage of this type of interview is that the researcher can easily compare the answers of the participants. The **semistructured interview** also typically has a set date and time with prearranged questions, yet the order of the questions is not strict and there is more participation in the discussion by the researcher. Depending on the flow of the interview, the researcher may also ask additional questions. In this way, the researcher has comparable questions and may also obtain unexpected information. The **unstructured interview** parallels a casual conversation with a member or members of the group under observation. However, the topics are primarily what the researcher is interested in at the time. The questions are not formally planned and the researcher may ask one participant one question and another participant a different question. The interview evolves based on the information offered in the process, meaning that the subject matter and the length of time of the interview may vary greatly from one participant to another.

Each type of interview has its advantages and disadvantages. The researcher therefore may use all three types of interviews during the research process in order to collect as much data as possible. Or, the researcher may follow particular theoretical and methodological paradigms that favor one type of interview over another. In any case, to conduct a productive interview, it is likely that the researcher will practice interviewing in advance so that the time is used wisely during the real interviews, the obtained information is clear, and the relationship with the participant stays intact.

thinking *critically*

What are some advantages and disadvantages of observation and interviews with respect to collecting data?

Field Notes

All of the information that the researcher gains from observations and interviews should be written down as field notes. The more time that passes between the interpersonal interactions and writing the information down the more likely it is that the data will be distorted based on the researcher's flawed memory. With good field notes, the researcher is better able to offer a realistic viewpoint and explanation of the social world in which the participants inhabit.

The **field notes** should be a chronological log similar to a personal journal, yet they should include several separate sections. One section should contain detailed descriptions of the observations and interviews without being intertwined with the researcher's guesses regarding the motivations or feelings of the participants. A second section should contain such interpretations and ideas about what is happening and why it is happening. A third section should contain the researcher's personal feelings—joys, sorrows, likes, dislikes, and so forth. The researcher's feelings may parallel the feelings of the participants. At the same time, keeping a log of personal feelings helps the researcher objectively see any potential biases that may distort the findings. Lastly, a fourth section should contain a list of things to do or questions to ask or descriptions of people and places to obtain in the future. Accomplishing all of this writing tends to take discipline and copious amounts of time, yet it is essential in order to gain a superior understanding of the social environment and the people who reside in it.

Step 4b: Analyzing the Data and Making Conclusions

Considering all of the details and components in the field notes, the amount of information that the researcher needs to analyze is typically substantial. Sorting through it may actually take more time than was spent in the field. A fundamental technique to simplify the evidence is to code it. **Coding** is the process of organizing the data into meaningful segments that can be logically linked together and easily accessible. Although a part of this process may involve creating themes out of the data, its primary purpose relates to the researcher's goals from the beginning—evaluating a program, testing a cause-and-effect relationship, or generating theory, for example. The initial step is to read through the field notes and group similar information together in relation to the study's goals. Many codes may be changed during the process and not all of the codes will be used in the final research report. Once several codes are identified, a more focused approach to coding may take place. The researcher groups several categories together to form analytical conclusions about what took place in the field and why.

In addition to the coding process, the researcher also writes descriptions, which are sometimes labeled **thick descriptions**, to illuminate the scene in which the participants live and act by covering the basic questions of who, what, where, and when. These descriptions may parallel a newspaper reporter's coverage of the social setting or a novelist's account of the social landscape. They offer a myriad of visual images, from a sense of place and smells to dramatic feelings and arguments. To a certain extent, the presentation of information may resemble a story with plots and characters, different points of views, and dialogue. It should grab the reader's attention. For example, here is the first line from Venkates's (2008) book *Gang Leader for a Day: A Rogue Sociologist Takes to the Streets*, which was a qualitative study of Chicago's urban poor: "I woke up at about 7:30 A.M. in a crack den, Apartment 1603 in Building Number 2301 of the Robert Taylor Homes." Even the opening line is descriptive and makes the reader want to know more, such as the reason he was in a crack den.

Finally, in order to further make sense of the dynamic aspects of the social setting and the human interplay that occurs within it, researchers create typologies and taxonomies. **Typologies** are general labels or concepts for people or activities that have similar characteristics, but may not be completely based on empirical evidence and do not range from specific to general. In college, some general labels would be fraternity guys, student-athletes, and good students. Since each individual within the social setting may fall under a number of classifications simultaneously, typologies are used to understand the intricacies of the broader social environment and people's place in it rather than determining any psychological attributes of specific individuals. **Taxonomies** also define groups based on shared characteristics but tend to increase from specificity to generalness and are typically based on empirical observation. What is helpful about taxonomies is that individuals can be grouped together and their relations may be mapped. For instance, person x may be a part of the family y, which belongs to the gang z, which is in competition with another gang, which has different families and individuals. Then, it may be clearer why person x gets into fights with person w in this particular social environment.

These are some of the techniques that qualitative sociologists use to draw conclusions from their collected data. Such studies are very powerful in their ability to decipher connections and meanings that take place in the real world. At the same time, because they are limited to a relatively small group of people, they are unable to offer conclusions about a larger population, which is the forte of quantitative research.

TRIANGULATION

Given that quantitative and qualitative methods have strengths and weaknesses, one strategy is to triangulate the research. **Triangulation** represents the idea of using different research methods to collect data on a single topic. For example, since quantitative methods are weak on discovering meaning, the qualitative techniques of observation and in-depth interviews could help to solve that problem. Because qualitative methods are limited to small, nonrandom groups of people, the quantitative technique of running surveys can test the qualitative findings with a larger, randomly selected group of people to represent the whole population. Another term that parallels the idea of triangulation is **mix-methods**, which favors using both quantitative and qualitative techniques in a research project. Although using mix-methods is valuable and preferable, most researchers tend to employ quantitative methods or qualitative methods but not both at the same time. The main reasons are practical rather than strategic. It costs a lot of money and takes a lot of time to use both methodologies.

JOB SKILLS: Solving Problems

Another skill that employers want in employees is the ability to solve problems. A Metlife survey found that 99 percent of employers considered problem-solving skills "essential" or "very important" for their businesses (Kay 2011). Mike Panigel, a senior vice president of human resources for the international corporation Siemens, says that a successful candidate will have the ability to quickly recognize the *key relationships* in a complex situation (Kay 2011).

Essentially, anyone who can do qualitative and quantitative research will satisfy Mr. Panigel's notion of problem solving, because that person will have the ability to identify a causal relationship and also have the knowledge of how to determine whether the causal relationship is supported by empirical evidence. For example, a general problem of many businesses is securing more clients.

How do we solve this problem? It is a cause-and-effect relationship. The effect is the potential client's acceptance or rejection of the business's services. What's the cause? It could be cost. Higher cost = reject services. It could be perception of services. The potential client may think that the services will not be helpful = reject services. It could be personality conflicts. The potential client may feel uncomfortable with the business's staff = reject services. It could be some other relationship or a combination of them. This is the type of thought pattern that leads to identifying *key relationships* and logical solutions to the problem. If cost is the problem, then offering discounts may help. If it is a mismatch in perceptions of services and desired services, then designing new ways to show the client how the business's services solve the client's problems may be beneficial. If personnel are the problem, staffing changes could net different results.

Yet, how do you know which relationship is the valid one in the situation? Qualitative methods suggest interviews and observation. Quantitative methods suggest surveys, perhaps with current clients to predict the potential client's needs and desires.

An attractive candidate for a job is one who knows the employer's problems and who also has ideas about solving the problems. Remember, the term *problem* does not always mean that something is wrong. Perhaps, it is more about solving the puzzle of increasing profits. *To practice, look at a company's website and brainstorm what problems it might have and how to solve them.*

RESEARCH ETHICS

Following an ethical code of conduct is essential for both quantitative and qualitative research. **Research ethics** refers to the notion that social scientists will act honestly in all aspects of the research process and will not consciously put their research subjects in danger or cause them any emotional or physical harm. In many cases, the scholars who work for colleges or universities must pass research proposals through an institutional review board (IRB) before beginning any projects. The American Sociological Association also has a specific code of ethics, which sociologists are supposed to follow when conducting their research. Given that sociologists study humans and that their work may have social, cultural, economic, and political ramifications, it is important that they act professionally and exercise as much forward-thinking behavior and sensitivity as possible.

SUMMARY

Sociologists follow the scientific method to collect their data. In particular, they begin by conducting a literature review on the topic of interest. Then, they use quantitative techniques, such as surveys and statistics, or qualitative techniques, such as observations and coding, to collect data. Some sociologists use mix-methods. In the end, they are able to obtain empirical evidence to test theories, to build theories, and to understand the meaning behind a host of perceptions and behaviors, all of which helps them find answers to their research questions about social reality. During this process, they also follow a research code of ethics to be fair-minded, truthful, and cognizant of the rights and dignities of their subjects, since their professional work may have significant implications for individuals and society.

Suggested Reading:

Creswell, John W. 2014. *Research Design: Qualitative, Quantitative, and Mixed Methods Approaches.* Thousand Oaks, CA: Sage Publications.

ACTIVE LEARNING PROJECTS

In Class:

1. Read a quantitative study from the journal *American Sociological Review* and identify the hypotheses, the dependent variables, the independent variables, the control variables, the sample, the findings, and the conclusions.
2. Read a qualitative study from the journal *Qualitative Research* and identify the type of observation used, the type of interviews conducted, the coding procedure used, any typologies or taxonomies created, and the conclusions.
3. Free write for a few minutes about a funny or embarrassing moment in your life. Then, take a few minutes and decide how you would study the reasons for, or causes of, the humor or embarrassment in this situation, using quantitative and qualitative methods.
4. In a small group, look through a magazine and identify some topics that could be researched and discuss how you could conduct the research as a research team.
5. In a small group, brainstorm a behavior in which men and women may differ (e.g., the number of times a person tries on clothing before going on a date) and ask people in the class to see if there is evidence for a difference between the two groups.

Out of Class:

1. Watch a video on YouTube.com and design a research project around the topic.
2. Visit a place in town that you have never been (e.g., a store, the farmer's market, a restaurant, a sporting event) and be a complete observer by taking field notes. Then, code your findings—that is, identify themes—and make conclusions about what is taking place in this social setting and why.
3. Watch a short clip of *What Would You Do?* on YouTube.com and write a 10-question survey that could be given to adults that would also gather information on the topic of the show's pseudo-experiment.
4. Identify a place where people leave public messages (e.g., bathroom stalls, Craigslist, abandoned buildings, personal ads in the newspaper) and record them to find any common themes.
5. Do a semistructured interview with a person who you admire and ask about his or her regrets in life and what the person would do differently if that were possible. So, prepare a list of questions, but also be ready to ask other questions based on the person's comments. Then, write an essay about the experience and findings.

KEY TERMS

Coding	Literature review	Simple random sampling
Complete observer	Longitudinal survey	Social construct
Complete participant	Macrosociology	Spurious relationship
Control variable	Microsociology	Structured interview
Convenient sample	Mix-methods	Surveys
Cross-sectional survey	Participant observer	Taxonomies
Dependent variable	Qualitative methods	Thick descriptions
Field notes	Quantitative methods	Triangulation
Hawthorne effect	Research ethics	Typologies
Hypothesis	Scientific method	Unstructured interview
Independent variable	Semistructured interview	Variable

PART III

How Do People Become
Social Beings?

chapter 5

Culture

- Culture is the totality of values, norms, beliefs, and symbols that are associated with certain people.
- Culture includes material and nonmaterial symbols.
- Subcultures and countercultures share specific cultural traits and practices that set them apart from the dominant culture, but the cultural traits and practices of countercultures are also at odds with the dominant culture.
- Ethnocentrism refers to the act of using one's own culture as the standard by which to judge other cultures.
- Cultural relativism is the idea that using another culture's perspective will aid in understanding the reasons behind that culture's behaviors without making judgments.

BE ABLE TO: Recognize ethnocentric tendencies and employ cultural relativism.

PEOPLE AND CULTURE

Before I studied abroad in Costa Rica, I went to an hour-long orientation on managing different cultural expectations. Throughout the whole lecture and discussion, the presenter drank from a beer bottle instead of a water bottle. It struck me as strange and made me uncomfortable. At the end, the presenter said that there was only water in the beer bottle. That was my first introduction to culture shock. **Culture shock** is the feeling of puzzlement and surprise that comes from experiencing a new and unfamiliar culture. All of us grow up in a social environment that has particular, taken-for-granted characteristics. We come to assume that the social patterns of behavior, the various symbols, and the whole way of life are normal, until we leave that environment and experience other traditions. This is culture: the subtle and overt expressions and behavioral customs, which incorporate the use of meaningful physical and nonphysical objects, and the accumulated and transmitted knowledge, that are linked to a particular group of people. Or, more succinctly, **culture** is the totality of values, norms, beliefs, and symbols associated with certain people.

The two general types of culture are material and nonmaterial. **Material culture** represents all of the tangible objects that humans make and give meaning to. Some of these things are cars, pets, and clothing. In the process, we also endow the objects with significance, even to the point of being willing to die for them. In the United States, many people see the American flag as a symbol of freedom and something to protect with their lives, even though ultimately it is just colored fabric, whereas in other places in the world, the American flag incites frustration, fear, and anger and is something to forfeit a life to fight against. This is similar with sacred texts, such as the Bible or Koran, which are fundamentally manufactured pieces of paper with type on them. But social groups endow these texts with enormous meaning. Many objects are critical in helping people fulfill their dreams, such as wedding attire. The occasions and clothes seem normal and taken-for-granted, but they differ drastically by country and without them the experience would have significantly less distinction.

The physical objects do not need to be constructed by humans. They can come from nature. The food we eat becomes cultural when we prepare it. We form a palate for certain foods, even though biologically our bodies are able to eat and enjoy a great variety of food. But over time we typically come to consider our food the best tasting in the world. For example, many college students in the United States crave hamburgers, pizza, pasta, fruits, ice cream, and cold cereal. Yet, in other countries, college students may point to other foods as delicious, such as rice, fish, beans, breads, and vegetables. Or, the objects may not have

any human preparation, but are still endowed with important meaning. Dogs, for example, have a relatively high position in U.S. culture, at least compared to other animals. Many people outside of the United States are astonished when they hear Americans say that they let their dogs sleep with them in bed or when Americans say that they would rather die than kill their dog if they were hypothetically alone in a cave without any other potential food source. The sociologist Clinton Sanders (2003) finds that Americans engage in identity-formation behaviors with their pets, such as giving them names, talking to them, and referring to them as one of the family, behaviors which at the same time also shape the pet owner's identity.

The other general type of culture is nonmaterial culture. **Nonmaterial culture** represents all of the nontangible features of human life. Language is a prime example of nonmaterial culture. Cultural differences are clearly visible among people from different societies, but they are also visible among people who reside in the same country, state, or community. For example, people who live in the upper Midwest to the West Coast in the United States often pronounce the word *pajamas* with "jam" in the middle (Hickey 2013). But people who live on the East Coast and in the South often pronounce the middle section with the "a" sounding similar to that in "father." Pa-jam-as versus pa-jah-mas. Some words also have a profound effect on whole nations. In the United States, for example, the general public and the court system have spent a vast number of hours discussing the definition of life in regard to fetal rights versus abortion rights. On the interpersonal level, many racially charged words have incited arguments and violence. Language is a monumental cultural force found in every society. Without it, we would lose our history, our ability to quickly and accurately communicate, and our ability to make sense of the world. In fact, some scholars argue that without language we might not be able to engage in higher order thinking. Other examples of nonmaterial culture include ideas and behavioral expectations about social life. Such things would include religious beliefs and expectations about morality. People have willingly given their time and even their lives for nonmaterial culture, such as debating the meaning of marriage or defining the status of a freedom fighter.

Values

A fundamental component of culture, specifically nonmaterial culture, is the set of values that a group of people develop. **Cultural values** are shared abstract ideas about what is right and wrong or good and bad. In societies, there may be some universal values while at the same time other values are disputed. In the United States, the notion that freedom and fairness are right and good is likely consistent across groups, even though the exact definition of each value may differ by groups. However, the idea that a woman should work outside the home in the labor market is held by some groups but not by other groups. Some groups consider a working mother to be productive for the nation and the family, while other groups consider it to be socially detrimental. In some cases, people may experience conflict when one value collides with another value. For example, in the education system, a person may ask a friend for the answers to a homework assignment or an exam, essentially asking the friend to cheat. The friend being asked is consequently put in a situation of moral conflict. It is right and good to avoid cheating. But it is also right and good to help a friend in need. Values are typically abstract, such as in the case of deciding what cheating or helping looks like, which makes them more guidelines of behavior rather than laws of behavior. In addition, values change over time when society changes, as happened through the civil rights movement, or when new generations with new ideas replace older generations that hold traditional ideas.

Norms

Norms are another important aspect of culture. Cultural **norms** are behaviors that groups consider to be expected and appropriate, which if violated have a sanction attached to them. This means that some behaviors may be considered inappropriate but do not invite negative reactions. These would not be considered norms. Many people today consider having a child out of wedlock to be undesirable, yet they do not ostracize the parent. The behavior of having children only within a marriage is less of a norm today than a decade ago. Norms tend to be invisible until they are broken. They come in three basic degrees. **Folkways** are the least consequential and have minor requirements for conformity. If you are at a restaurant on a first date with someone and you use your fork to take a piece of food off of his or her plate without permission, you are likely going to receive a disapproving look or comment from your date

"The new guy is great for morale, but he's clueless about the dress code."

since sharing food with someone without asking typically comes later in the relationship. **Mores** are more consequential and if broken may result in loss of relationships or jail time. These also may differ based on social status, including race, gender, class, age, and sexual orientation. For example, a male college student who walks around campus shirtless may be breaking a folkway but a female college student would be breaking a more and could be given a ticket. The number of folkways and mores is extremely large and the number varies from group to group and year to year. **Taboos** are the most consequential and if broken may lead to capital punishment. Some examples of taboos include murder, cannibalism, and terrorism. Many norms, especially mores and taboos, are formalized into law so that violations of conformity will have legal as well as social ramifications.

Beliefs

Cultural beliefs are shared ideas about reality. They are not referring to ideas about what is right and wrong, such as the statement "I believe that all persons under 18 should receive an education." Even though this statement has the term "believe" in it, it would not be considered a cultural belief. An example of a cultural belief is: "I believe that all people under the age of 18 lack experience in life." This comment refers to a state of being rather than an ideal. The validity of the belief is irrelevant. For example, many people believe that the theory of evolution reflects the reality of how humans became humans, and many people also believe in a conscious life after their body ceases to exist on earth. Both are beliefs about reality, notwithstanding a range in scientific support. On the social side of things, other beliefs would include ideas about certain social groups. Whites are good politicians. African Americans are good athletes. Asian Americans are intelligent. The validity of these ideas may be more or less correct based on empirical evidence, but they remain reflections of cultural beliefs.

Symbols

Values, norms, and beliefs are also signified by cultural symbols. **Cultural symbols** are physical and nonphysical objects that are endowed with meaning to represent something other than themselves. When a lover presents a rose, he or she is not offering a plant but rather is communicating affection. When a sports fan yells to a player, "You rock!" he or she is not calling the player a hard stone or commanding the player to shake back and forth but is conveying his or her support and praise. Cultural symbols are everywhere, from planted trees to skyscrapers, and people are often unaware of them on an intellectual level. For example, clothes are cultural symbols that represent an enormous amount of information about taste, class, race, gender, and age, among other things. Yet, most people probably do not spend the majority of their time analyzing all of these different aspects to their clothes. One reason many activists criticize the high-end fashion world for putting excessively skinny models down the runway is because they believe women unconsciously develop an unhealthy body image. In many cases, however, the decision makers regarding fashion models are not using the fashion models to communicate anything to the general public but rather to other fashion insiders who have specific cultural norms and values that may not be shared by the general public (Mears 2009). The cultural symbols therefore are pervasive, powerful, and often interpreted differently by different groups of people.

CHECK POINT: What is culture?

SUBCULTURES AND COUNTERCULTURES

Some groups of people are set apart from the rest of society because of their culture. **Subcultures** are groups of people that have specific cultural norms, values, and beliefs that are different or more intense from the rest of society but not counter to society. Such groups would include certain occupations, such as mortuary workers and police offers, certain religious groups, such as the Amish, and certain racial and ethnic groups, from Asian Americans to Puerto Ricans. Other subcultures may be based on factors like age, sexual orientation, political ideology, or even interest in particular hobbies. **Countercultures** are groups

of people that share cultural norms, values, and beliefs that are perceived by the larger society, or at least the powerful groups in the larger society, to be at odds with the dominant culture or threatening in some way. In the past, it may have been Communists, the Ku Klux Klan, or hippies, while a more current example could be Muslims or undocumented immigrants.

In some cases, these smaller cultural groups may be problematic or legitimately dangerous for society. However, members of the dominant cultural group may be expressing ethnocentrism. **Ethnocentrism** is the act of assuming one's own culture is superior and the standard by which other cultures should be judged. Other cultures consequently tend to appear lacking in quality. In contrast to ethnocentrism, many scholars argue that we should attempt to evaluate and understand other cultures using the other cultures' perspectives. This is **cultural relativism**—the belief that the only way to understand other cultures is to view those other cultures from their own cultural context. For example, when I was living in the Philippines, a large number of Filipinos complained to me that Americans are cruel to their elders because Americans put their elders in residential living centers separated from their families. In the Philippines, it is common for many generations in a family to live together, and when I was there it was easy to see that in their society such living arrangements offered a great amount of support and enjoyment. At the same time, the social structural aspects of the United States make such intergenerational living arrangements less feasible and, in the opinion of many Americans, less desirable for the elderly. Due to the economy, many Americans are forced to move around for jobs and many are forced to live in residential spaces that do not have the living space for their older family members. Additionally, the residential living centers have access to food preparers and hospital care. Ultimately, children and parents who grow up in the United States greatly endorse the cultural value of independence, making the notion of living away from adult children typical and expected for the elderly. Therefore, to understand the behaviors of a society it helps to use that society's cultural perspective.

thinking *critically*

What do people mean when they say we are in a "culture war" and to what extent is this cultural war positive or negative for society?

JOB SKILLS: Being Culturally Aware and Building Cultural Capital

In the current period, more and more employers are consciously trying to diversify their workforce. They are doing this for a couple of reasons. One is because a diverse workforce brings in different perspectives that may offer an advantage to the business. Another reason is that, as the world becomes more interconnected due to technology and globalization, businesses are dealing with financiers, clients, and competitors from across the globe. Having a workforce that can understand cultural differences is likely to give the business a competitive edge. Employees who understand the idea of cultural relativism—the notion of using a culture's own perspective to judge its members' behaviors—are likely to be valued by growing businesses.

Building up a reservoir of cultural knowledge will give you what the French sociologist Pierre Bourdieu called "**cultural capital**," which is the cultural knowledge of the norms, values, beliefs, and practices of a group of people, especially the group in power. Someone who knows a potential client's cultural preferences in food, for example, can use that knowledge in exchange for a better relationship. Similarly, an employee with cultural capital can use his or her cultural knowledge to better existing relations with coworkers and bosses. Be open to new cultural experiences to build up your cultural capital and it may just pay off in the end in terms of professional advancement.

SUMMARY

Culture is so pervasive that we experience it and perform it every day, all day. In particular, we express values of right and wrong and follow norms of expected behavior. We also hold certain beliefs about reality and use symbols to communicate. Some groups of people share material and nonmaterial aspects of culture that set them apart from the mainstream culture, and thereby create subcultures and countercultures. In order to better understand cultural groups, it is productive to curtail ethnocentric tendencies, which place one's own culture as the standard by which all other cultures should be judged, and to instead employ the notion of cultural relativism, which argues that unfamiliar cultures are best understood through their own cultural perspectives.

Suggested Reading:

Mears, Ashley. 2010. "Size Zero High-end Ethnic: Cultural Production and the Reproduction of Culture in Fashion Modeling." *Poetics* 38:21-46.

ACTIVE LEARNING PROJECTS

In Class:

1. Free write what you had to do in the morning to get ready and discuss the similarities and differences with a person of the opposite sex, exploring why differences exist.
2. Draw the first image that comes to mind when you hear the words "fraternity guy," "marriage," "food," and "transportation," and, in a small group, discuss how and why you pictured these images.
3. Watch the video *Killing Us Softly* and in a small group discuss its main points, the extent to which the video's message can relate to your social world, and the extent to which you agree with its arguments.
4. In a small group, each tell a joke and discuss what are the cultural values, norms, and beliefs that make the jokes funny.
5. Free write some traditions you do during the holidays or for birthdays and identify the important cultural symbols and what they mean for you.

Out of Class:

1. Research a counterculture and describe the characteristics that make it a counterculture.
2. Listen to a popular song on the radio and explain what it is telling us about U.S. cultural values, norms, and beliefs.
3. Research online mores and taboos that people in the United States would not want to violate but people in other countries consider to be acceptable behavior, such as differences in food choices or male–female relationship practices.
4. Write an essay on what you imagine would be the most shocking about U.S. society to a foreigner. That is, what would the foreign person's experiences of culture shock entail?
5. Pick a topic that is controversial in the United States (e.g., abortion, immigration, same-sex marriage), describe the arguments from both sides, and identify the foundational cultural values, norms, and beliefs of each side.

KEY TERMS

Countercultures	Culture	Nonmaterial culture
Cultural beliefs	Culture shock	Norms
Cultural capital	Ethnocentrism	Subcultures
Cultural relativism	Folkways	Taboos
Cultural symbols	Material culture	
Cultural values	Mores	

chapter 6

Socialization

- Socialization is the process by which people learn the cultural norms, values, beliefs, and practices of the social environment in which they participate.
- Charles Horton Cooley coined the term "looking-glass self," explaining it as the process by which individuals develop a social self through reflecting on what they believe others think of them.
- George Herbert Mead advanced notions of socialization with his concepts of the "me," the "I," the play, and the generalized other.
- Erving Goffman added to the notion that socialization is a lifelong process with his dramaturgical approach.
- There are many formal agents of socialization, including the family, education system, mass media, the workplace, and the government.

BE ABLE TO: Identify some of the processes of socialization in your community.

PROCESS OF SOCIALIZATION

Every morning millions of people go through a routine of getting ready for the day. They likely shower, get dressed, and eat breakfast. Then, they leave their residence and interact with a variety of other people, until they return home, eat dinner, and perform their nightly routine of going to bed. Day after day, they do these things, and most of them probably do it without giving it much thought. Why is it easy? One answer is that we have all been socialized to our society's way of life. **Socialization** is the process by which people learn the cultural norms, values, beliefs, and practices of the social environment in which they participate. From the very first day of life—some scholars may even argue from the time in the womb—individuals learn how to be members of a group or larger community. It is worth noting that an individual does not learn everything there is to learn, but rather that which is designated as appropriate for his or her social situation. For example, at the University of Idaho, a student club often sets up a booth called "Walk a Mile in Her Shoes" in order to generate awareness about gender inequality. Watching the male students, especially the male athletes, put on high heels and promenade down the pathway makes everyone laugh. None of them can walk 10 feet without stumbling. Everyone knows that it is not because they lack physical ability. They were simply not trained to wear those types of shoes. As another example, during the day individuals typically communicate with both men and women, with friends and people in authority positions, and with strangers. Do these individuals act the same way around each of the different types of people? Unlikely. We communicate and behave differently when we are with friends compared to when we are with our boss or a stranger. Often, our clothing is carefully selected so as to be appropriate for a specific interaction, such as job interviews. How do we know how to make these adjustments? Were we born with this knowledge? Did we read it in a book? We gained this competency through agents of socialization.

NATURE VERSUS NURTURE

An ongoing debate in popular media revolves around whether our actions are based on biology or society. My guess is that most scholars today would accept that the answer involves a combination of the two. There are predispositions based in biology that influence the way a person behaves and the way that a person views life as he or she ages. For example, some researchers are finding evidence that our political ideologies, be they conservative or liberal or something else, likely have their fundamental origins in our genes, hormone levels, and neurotransmitter systems (Buchen 2012). On an anecdotal level, parents of more than one child are frequently amazed by how significantly different each of their children are from one another in terms of personality, tastes, and behavior, even though the parents' lifestyles and parenting did not appear to change significantly. Biology would seem to play an important role in these differences.

The question for sociologists, however, is: How does a person go from being a biological being to a social being? Prior research has shown that people who grow up with little to no human interaction are impeded in terms of maturation, brain development, language acquisition, and social ability (Newton 2004). Society also plays an important role in people's lives. Fortunately, most people, regardless of their political orientations or general taste differences, know how to interact successfully with other people. Even behaviors that may be considered purely biological, such as experiencing hunger, elicit varying responses from people depending on the society. People eat different foods and eat with particular people based on cultural expectations. Sociologists are interested in the what, when, with who, why, where, and how of individual behavior and interpersonal interaction—all which is influenced by the social environment.

DEVELOPMENT OF THE SOCIAL SELF

For over a century, scientists have theorized about the process of becoming a social being. Sociologist **Charles Horton Cooley** (1864–1929) posited the idea that we gain a social identity by interacting with other people, as opposed to being born with a social identity. He used the term **looking-glass self**. A looking-glass is another word for a mirror. With this term, he argued that people create a social identity by determining what they think other people think of them. People see themselves in the eyes and behaviors of other people, as if other people were the mirror. If Julie believes that her family and friends think that she is intelligent, then Julie comes to think of herself as intelligent and acts accordingly. If Hector thinks that his schoolteachers and community consider him to be a hard worker, he sees himself as a hard worker and acts accordingly.

Cooley's theoretical ideas outline such outcomes as a process consisting of three stages. First, people imagine how they appear to other people, from parents to strangers. Second, people come to a conclusion about the ways other people assessed them—for example, attractive, funny, or ambitious. Third, people experience a degree of pride or shame from these interactions and perceptions. This reflective process typically occurs internally, but it shapes the person's identity and how he or she will act with others. It is the constant frequency of particular interactions over time and with a variety of people that matter. For instance, during childhood, a boy's impression of what his mother thinks of him tends to be more powerful than what he believes his friends think of him. But once he reaches adolescence, the power of these relationships may switch.

Another important aspect of Cooley's theoretical ideas is that the person may be incorrect about other peoples' assessments. A coach may tell a player to be confident on the field. The player may then think that the coach believes that the player is not confident, and then the player comes to believe that he or she is in fact not confident in his or her abilities. Yet, the coach may not have been evaluating the player's level confidence at all but rather

"It makes you look forty years younger."

just trying to rally the player. Regardless, the process of the looking-glass self had been initiated and effectual. Bronson (2007) summarizes research showing that when children are told that they are smart, they are likely to quickly give up on something that they perceive to be difficult, while children who are told that they are hard workers are likely to struggle for a solution and even find the problem enjoyable. In one of the experiments, the students who were told that they were smart did not want to appear unintelligent and so they immediately quit. The other students who were told that they worked hard had no social identity about being smart in that situation and consequently liked the challenge.

George Herbert Mead (1863–1931) elaborated on Cooley's theoretical ideas to form another theory about the way socialization works in shaping a person's social identity. He argued that people develop the "**Me**," which is a concept that represents what an individual believes others think of him or her, and the "**I**," which is a concept that represents the individual's personal identity. Some scholars refer to this as the objective self, seeing the self through the eyes of other people as if the self were an object, and the subjective self, the internal part of the person. These two aspects of the self often interact: "What will he think of *me* if *I* wear that?" Mead also argued that people develop a social self in stages. The *play stage* occurs in childhood when children take on the roles of other people, such as pretending to be a doctor, a superhero, or a mommy. They learn to use cultural symbols and to communicate their social identity to other people. There are no set rules, except for the ones that the children make up as they play. Then children move on to the *game stage*, where they engage in games that involve multiple players and multiple roles and have objective rules. In this stage, they come to understand the expectations of their role in isolation but also the expectations of their role in contrast to another person's role. Consequently, they learn how to comprehend the necessary actions of somebody else in relation to themselves in order to have successful interactions. In a game of baseball, they may take on the role of the batter while understanding the role

"What do I have to do, start drowning, to get the lifeguard to look at me?!"

© 2014 Cartoonresource. Used under license of Shutterstock, Inc.

of the pitcher. These conceptions then extend to other social situations, such as sitting in a restaurant. They know when and how they are supposed to order food and they can imagine how the server views them and what the server likely expects of them. By the end of the game stage, the individual is capable of interacting with a diverse set of people in different parts of the overall social environment.

Mead went on to describe another important concept: the generalized other. The **generalized other** consists of the perceived expectations, attitudes, and viewpoints of the whole community. The generalized other is constantly in the mind of the social self, and influences a people's interactions with others. Not only do these social selves recognize their own role and that of the others in their social environment but they also consider what society in general might expect and think. Passing through these stages and acquiring these abilities and knowledge results in people developing social selves.

Socialization, in the sense of learning how to interact as a social being in society, does not end in childhood or young adulthood. It is a process that occurs over the entire life course. **Erving Goffman** (1922–1982) added another dimension to the theories of socialization with his **dramaturgical approach**. In this theoretical framework, Goffman argues that context and audience are important aspects of selfhood. Taken from Shakespeare's notion of *all the world is a stage*, it is assumed that we are all actors playing a role in a particular context at a certain time for a specific audience. Goffman argued that there is a front stage, where people know other people are watching them and expecting something, and a backstage, which is a comparatively private place. In both locations, but particularly when on front stage, people create a **definition of the situation**. In other words, they come to define the context as being filled with certain norms, values, symbols, and interpersonal connections. They set up the stage in their minds to have certain actors playing known roles with recognizable symbols. A court of law, a classroom, and a party are all metaphorical stages wherein the definition of the situation is likely easy to ascertain and shared by other people, making a person's social identity comprehensible in those arenas. However, misunderstanding and conflict may occur when two people attempt to define the situation differently. In a game of tennis, one person may define the situation as a competitive match while the other person may define it as a time to have fun, resulting in frustration for both people involved. Another example is when one partner in a romantic couple defines a restaurant as a place to have a serious conversation about the relationship while the other partner defines the restaurant as a front stage location and feels uncomfortable discussing what he or she may consider backstage matters.

thinking *critically*

While in the social situation, people are also creating a **presentation of self**. With this concept, Goffman was highlighting the idea that people attempt to appear a certain way by using symbols and gestures. They engage in **impression management**—the action of trying to present a self that pleases the audience. The contemporary sociologist, Elijah Anderson, discussed the presentation of self of inner-city residents in his book, *The Code of the Street*. The inner-city residents that he studied wore particular clothing, made certain movements, and spoke in a specific way. It all added up to a presentation of self that attempted to garner respect in the public sphere and ward off confrontation. To attain one of the desirable symbols, such as a certain pair of shoes or a hat, amplified the person's presentation of self and boosted the person's status in the social situation. It was a form of communication. But a person had to learn the code to understand the message. Ultimately, people in every social environment are constantly in the process of socialization. We are forced to discover the workings of a new social environment. When someone enters a new town, school, place of employment, relationship, or any other unfamiliar social context, he or she is socialized to that environment's values, norms, beliefs, and practices.

CHECK POINT: What is socialization and how does one develop a social self?

AGENTS OF SOCIALIZATION

The social structural entities in society that socialize people on a grand scale are called **agents of socialization**. The family and peer networks are important ones because they are usually the first to teach people how to be social beings. Other agents of socialization include voluntary associations, such as religions and social movements, and institutions, such as the media and the workplace. Some agents of socialization are state mandated, such as the education system and the state and federal governments. Each agent of socialization teaches people something different and reflects the complex web of society. Finally, they also help with resocializing people when needed. Many people, for example, return to college after long careers in the labor market. They want to update their skills and in the process are resocialized to the new environments. Another place where **resocialization** occurs is in **total institutions**, which are organizations that separate people out from society and engage in powerful, formalized tactics of socialization. The military is an example. Young adults enter the military having been socialized into a civil life. Once inside, however, their lives are quickly controlled. Their appearance is changed, including hairstyle and clothing, and they are made to perform specific jobs in a defined social hierarchy. They are taught what to do and with whom to interact. They are trained under intense conditions. Eventually they are resocialized in a manner that is satisfactory to the military leadership. At the same time, parts of the prior socialization of civilian life never leave them, just as parts of a military life never leave them once they have completed their service and returned to civilian life.

JOB SKILLS: Acclimating to the Workplace

When workers enter a new job, they quickly discover that there is a "way" of doing things. A coworker may formally train them, or they may have to learn as they go. They are eventually socialized to the culture of the workplace to the point where most things become familiar and seem normal. As a future employee it will be helpful to recognize that this process may not be easy and it may take time. Furthermore, as an employee or manager, understanding this process and instituting policies or strategies to help workers acclimate to the new social environment is likely to be worthwhile for everyone. When you entered a new school, what did you have or experience or wished you had or experienced to help you feel comfortable quickly?

SUMMARY

Socialization is the process by which people learn the cultural norms, values, beliefs, and practices of the social environment in which they participate. Two of the major sociologists who explained this process were Charles Horton Cooley, who defined the looking-glass self as the process of developing a social self by determining what other people think, and George Herbert Mead, who advanced the concepts of the Me and the I in addition to arguing that people go through the developmental stages of play and game. He also discussed the concept of the generalized other, which is the perception of what the whole community thinks. As people learn to take on roles in the play stage, then learn their roles relative to other people's roles in the game stage, and finally incorporate the generalized other, they become social selves. Erving Goffman added to the theories of socialization by arguing that roles are enacted in particular contexts and at certain times in front of specific audiences. People come to define situations and present themselves in ways that they believe will please their audiences. Finally, formal agents of socialization, such as the family and education system, teach people how to behave and interact throughout their lives.

Suggested Reading:

Sanders, Clinton R. 2003. "Actions Speaker Louder than Words: Close Relationships between Humans and Nonhuman Animals." *Symbolic Interaction* 26:405-426.

ACTIVE LEARNING PROJECTS

In Class:

1. Write about a moment in childhood when you felt like you really began to take on your own identity.
2. Write a letter to your 16-year-old self with respect to ways to make life easier or better.
3. Watch the video *Mickey Mouse Monopoly* and, in a small group, discuss its main arguments and the extent to which you believe them and why.
4. In a small group, identify places and topics that may be considered front stage and backstage and why.
5. Write about the agent of socialization that you believe has had the most impact on you and why.

Out of Class:

1. Look through magazines targeted at women and men and identify how they are socializing people to present themselves to others.
2. Identify things that a loved one did for you while growing up that helped you and write them a letter about it.
3. Go to a public place and observe people from a dramaturgical perspective, identifying definitions of the situation, presentations of self, impression management, and front stage/backstage actions.
4. Write a reflection paper that describes your greatest strengths and weaknesses, and explain how you came to believe these qualities about yourself.
5. Research some of the parenting strategies that parents use in another country which are different from your experience and brainstorm in writing some of the implications for the children and the society.

KEY TERMS

Agents of socialization	Goffman, Erving	Mead, George Herbert
Cooley, Charles Horton	The I	Presentation of self
Definition of the situation	Impression management	Resocialization
Dramaturgical approach	Looking-glass self	Socialization
Generalized other	The Me	Total institution

chapter 7

Aging and the Life Course

KEEP IN MIND

- Aging is the process of growing older biologically and passing through a number of socially constructed life course stages and relationships.
- There are four general types of aging: chronological aging, functional aging, social roles and aging, and subjective aging.
- There are numerous theories of aging, ranging from micro to macro in level.
- The life course perspective implies that personal decisions and events that occur at one point in time will have lasting consequences throughout a person's life.
- The population of people 65 years old and older continues to grow and have societal implications.

BE ABLE TO: Remember the four different types of aging and recognize them in your own life.

WHEN YOU ARE OLD

When you are old and grey and full of sleep,
And nodding by the fire, take down this book,
And slowly read, and dream of the soft look
Your eyes had once, and of their shadows deep;

How many loved your moments of glad grace,
And loved your beauty with love false or true,
But one man loved the pilgrim soul in you,
And loved the sorrows of your changing face;

—William Butler Yeats

For me, the first two stanzas of this poem by Yeats concisely characterize the wonderful joys and sadness of aging, and, in the end, as Yeats implies, aging is essentially recognized through a person's relationships from the past and present. In less poetic terms, **aging** is the process of growing older biologically and passing through a number of socially constructed life course stages and relationships. It is likely that when most people define the word "age" they immediately refer to a set number of years of life, which are predicated on a sense of time measured by the revolution of the earth around the sun and the corresponding physical maturation and decline of humans. Although this is one important conception of age, the idea of aging is much more complex and social.

FOUR CATEGORIES OF AGING

There are at least four general categories of aging (Quadagno 2011). **Chronological aging** is the numeric, time-dependent conception of aging. Birthdays are an annual reminder of this form of aging. Societies also use this type of aging to formalize rules that they consider socially important, such as the age when someone can drive a car, join the military, drink alcohol, get married, enter a political office, join certain voluntary associations for retired people, and be eligible for age-dependent government benefits. In the United States, the typical age designations over the life course are 0 to 17 for children, 18 to 64 for adults, and 65 and over for older adults. At the same time, chronological age can be an inappropriate indicator of aging. Someone who is 65 is likely to be comparatively similar to someone who falls in the adult category and comparatively dissimilar to someone who is aged 85.

Additionally, many people who are advanced in chronological age are healthier and more active than a large percentage of people who claim a younger age. Some people who are younger than the legal age for drinking alcohol are more responsible with its use and more tolerant of its effects than many people who are older than the legal age. Chronological age therefore is only a starting point to understanding age and aging.

Functional aging refers to the objective actions a person can accomplish and the subjective perceptions of how a person looks. If a young person is able to compete physically or intellectually with older individuals, he or she is considered old for his or her years. Similarly, if an older person is able to remain active at work or doing various youthful activities, he or she may be considered young. At the same time, many young people are thought of as old based on their appearance while many older people are considered young because of their appearance. One of the consequences of these appearances is that the individuals experience different social interactions and consequently behave differently, which may ultimately lead to self-fulfilling prophecies regarding being young or old. If someone appears older than their age and is unable to accomplish the tasks typical for his or her age group, the resulting social interactions may acerbate the person's appearance and functional ability. On the other hand, a young person who has an older appearance may actually gain more respect or have more opportunities to be a functioning member of society, leading to even greater opportunities. In either case, the aging process is influenced by a person's objective and subjective functionality.

These ideas relate to the next type of aging: **social roles and aging**. Social roles are the behaviors people are supposed to enact when they take on a specific status. An adult is supposed to be independent from other people with respect to living outside his or her family of origin. A retiree is supposed to stop working. Playing these roles may have consequences for how someone ages. A 25-year-old woman with two children will age differently than a 25-year-old woman with no children. They will participate in different activities; be expected by family, friends, and society to do different things; and likely hold different perspectives on a variety of issues. Some of the social roles are also entered into nonvoluntarily. For example, a person who has children around the age of 20 may become a grandparent around the age of 40, and the role of being a grandparent may make that person feel older and consequently restrict his or her activities in a way that a 40-year-old person who is not a grandparent might not do. Social roles, therefore, also influence how we age over a lifetime.

Along these lines, **subjective aging** is based on the idea of how old one feels. Many people that society may categorize as old often express the sentiment that they actually feel much younger than their chronological age. Or, they might say that they are young at heart. On the other end of the age spectrum, young people often feel older than their chronological age and sometimes assume that other people consider them to be older, too. A large number of factors can affect a person's subjective age. People from the upper classes tend to take longer to feel older, while people from the working classes tend to feel older sooner. Racial minorities are more likely to feel older sooner than Whites. Health issues quickly make people feel older. These feelings blur the categorical lines drawn by chronological age.

Aging is much more of a multidimensional process than a birth year would indicate. These other forms of aging help explain why everyone of the same chronological age does not age in the same way or feel the same way. Although it is clear that biology influences aging, society also plays a major role in the aging process.

CHECK POINT: What are the four general types of aging?

THEORIES OF AGING

© 2014 Binkski. Used under license of Shutterstock, Inc.

Similar to other substantive topics in sociology, the theories of aging range from micro to mezzo to macro in scale. **Micro theories** focus specifically on individuals. To begin with, there is a number of **biological theories** that explain why people age. The *wear and tear theory* intuitively argues that our bodies are like machines and that after a lot of use, they wear down, break apart, and deteriorate. Our sleep patterns change. Our sensory organs are less able to provide information for us. Our bones become weaker. Over time, we just naturally decline in physical and mental ability. The *cross-linkage theory* states that our cells are composed of collagen, which binds cells together and looks like cross-links. But during the early years in life, people do not have many cross-links. As people age, they develop more and more cross-links that harden the tissue, making flexibility and blood circulation worse. Eventually, the body diminishes. The *free radical theory* says that we have helpful molecules and unhelpful ones, such as the free radicals. They take the energy from the productive molecules, leading to the body feeling tired and weak. They are also associated with various forms of cancer and Alzheimer's disease. Antioxidants reduce the number of free radicals in the body. Therefore, people who eat fruits, berries, and vegetables are likely to remain comparatively healthy because they have antioxidants controlling the detrimental effects of free radicals. This process would explain the variation in aging among people. Lastly, the *genetic control theory* argues that a large part of our aging process is predisposed in our genes. Our genes may decide the likelihood of experiencing life-threatening diseases, which may constrain longevity. One criticism of these theories, however, is that they help to explain why the body fades over time but they do not speak to the reason why we age the way that we do in the social world. Furthermore, they ignore evidence that indicates that interaction with other people stimulates biological responses in humans, which can help or hinder the physical aging of individuals.

There are also social theories that focus on the individual. **Disengagement theory** was one of the early explanations of the patterns of aging. It argued that people follow a natural pathway of aging that goes from being connected to the social world and all of its activities to withdrawing from society and limiting interactions with other people. People take on fewer roles, such as work and parenthood, as they age. Both the aging person and society approve of this separation, it is argued. The older person has less responsibility and less stress and can prepare for death. For society, as older individuals disengage, there is room for younger people to take their place. New business employees, new teachers, new politicians, and so forth can all add fresh ideas to social systems and advance social progress. Critics

of this theory, however, argue that a large portion of the population does not disengage from society and a large portion does not want to disengage, meaning that the trend of disengagement is neither natural nor desirable for many people.

Activity theory suggests that as people age, they remain the same as younger people in terms of desires for activity and interaction. To some extent, physical aging may constrain certain activities but older individuals do not want to withdraw from or shrink their social world. Some research finds that older individuals who are the most active are happiest and least likely to fall into depression (Quadagno 2011). Being active, as in childhood and adulthood, is the way to age into old age as well. Nonetheless, critics of this theory revert back to disengagement theory and argue that there are people who disengage and want to curtail their social worlds. Consequently, activity theory is also limited in its ability to explain the aging process. Scholars currently accept that there is diversity in the aging process and now attempt to explain when and why some people disengage and other people remain active.

Mezzo theories incorporate the idea that interactions with other people affect a person's aging process. It is not solely the individual who decides how he or she will age. **Exchange theory** makes the case that people engage in exchange relationships with

"Woman of a certain age, meet man at a particular time in life."

other people and that this process affects the individual's type of aging. The assumption is that people are rational actors and want to maximize their benefits and minimize their costs. It is argued that one reason that there is relatively more interaction between people similar in age and comparatively less interaction between younger and older people is because there is more and less to exchange, respectively. Yet, as older people have more to exchange, such as money, time, wisdom, and other resources, they are likely to have a greater amount of interaction with a wider range of people, including family, friends, and acquaintances who can help them emotionally and physically, resulting in a difference in the aging process compared to someone who has less to exchange and therefore experiences less interaction and help. One criticism of this approach is that not all interactions follow a rational choice and transactional system, especially when dealing with loved ones. We often base our interactions on feelings and emotions rather than on a cost-benefit analysis, suggesting that people will interact even when it is more costly and emotionally draining to do so. Not all social interactions may have a positive impact on the aging process.

thinking *critically*

How might exchange theory explain why some people disengage from society and other people remain active until they pass away?

Social constructionism is a theoretical framework that takes a different approach to explaining the aging process. It argues that people construct their realities through social interaction, making the meaning they give to objects and behaviors critical to understanding any topic. Since social interaction and created meaning are at the center of this theoretical idea, the implication is that social outcomes are situational and dynamic. With reference to aging, people understand the aging process based on the meaning they give to it as a result of their interactions with other people. For example, when college students are with their friends, they may feel like adults. Yet, when they return home for the holidays and interact with their parents, they may feel less adult-like, even though their chronological age did not change. The social interactions and the meanings of age derived from the interactions with the two different sets of people led to different perceptions of the aging process. Critics of this approach, however, argue that it ignores the effects of social structural powers such as religion, the government, and the media to influence the aging process and the meanings people give to age.

Macro theories focus on the larger structural conditions of society to explain individuals' aging process. **Age integration theory** suggests that societies are stratified by age. High school is typically reserved for persons younger than 18, while residential living centers are typically reserved for persons older than 55. Therefore, some social institutions are age-segregated, where one age group is unable to receive the same privileges and resources as another age group. Yet, society also has age-integrated institutions. The family and the workplace are age-integrated institutions because they often consist of people of varying ages. To the extent that people reside or work in either an age-segregated or age-intergraded institution, they will experience their aging process differently because the social institutions have an impact on the ability to disengage or be active, engage in exchange relations with certain people, and create meaning with respect to age. One of the main criticisms of this theory, however, is that it ignores the intersecting dimensions of other forms of stratification, such as race, gender, and class. A woman is likely to have a very different experience than a man in the same institution, such as the family or workplace, leading to differences in the aging process.

A **critical gerontology approach** argues that scholars must examine global dynamics to understand the aging process of individuals. Global politics, economics, and culture are foundational to stratification systems, exchange relations, and individual behavior. For example, financial institutions around the world are interconnected. Depending on interactions between these financial institutions, interest rates may go up or down, resulting in borrowing costs that influence health insurance companies, which change their policies based on the interest rates. This change then affects individuals and their aging process. One of the main criticisms of these macro approaches is that they disregard the individual's ability to adapt and the ability to create meaning out of the situation and respond creatively.

CHECK POINT: Give an example of one micro, one mezzo, and one macro theory of aging?

LIFE COURSE PERSPECTIVE

The life course perspective incorporates ideas from all three theoretical levels, from micro to mezzo to macro. The **life course perspective** has several tenets: (1) Humans are free to make decisions and construct their lives, but are simultaneously influenced by (2) their dependence on other people and (3) the social structures of their community and society during specific historical time periods while they are a particular age (Sampson and Laub 2003). For example, the sociologist Glen Elder (1974) notes that the age group that passed through the Great Depression with the best future prospects were children who were preteens, around ages 9 through 12. They were not too young to have their lives and bodies severally changed by the depression and they were not too old to have to struggle through the enormous stress and deprivation. At the same time, they came into adulthood during World War II, but were at the right age to enjoy the booming economy afterward—again not too young and not too old. Because of their choices, dependence on others, and age during certain macro-structural events, such as economic busts and booms, it worked out better for them, compared to other age groups. One important implication is that the choices and events that affect people at one point in time during their lives will have lasting consequences throughout their lives.

CHECK POINT: What are the tenets of the life course perspective?

TRANSITION TO ADULTHOOD

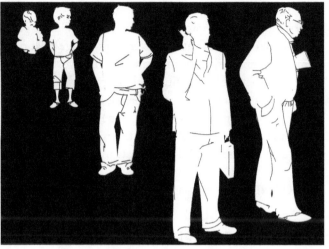

Would you say that you always feel like an adult? People between the ages of 18 and 30 often say that they feel like an adult only some of the time. Many scholars are currently studying the factors that lead to someone feeling like an adult and being considered an adult. From psychology, Jeffery Arnett (2000) argues that individuals come up with their own conception of what an adult looks like and what an adult does. Some examples of these characteristics are making financial decisions, deciding on political and religious beliefs, and living outside the family of origin. Then, the individual evaluates oneself in comparison to a self-conception of adulthood. The more characteristics the person believes that he or she shares with this image of adulthood the more likely the person will feel like an adult and be considered an adult by other people. Arnett argues that for young people in Western countries this **transition to adulthood** takes many years. So the group of people between ages 18 and 30 often do not consider themselves adolescents nor adults. They are in a state of transition, which he called **emerging adulthood**.

Sociologists often examine the influences that come from the social environment to explain when and why someone transitions into adulthood. In many cases, they focus on the social markers and roles of adulthood: leaving the family of origin, finishing school, having a career, getting married, and having a child. They argue that, as people enter into more of these roles, they come to feel like adults, consider themselves to be adults, and have other people treat them like adults. In addition, sociologists explore the effects of social context. These young people are likely to perceive themselves to be adults at different times depending on their locations—in college, in the workplace, at home with parents, at a party, or someplace else. They argue that self-perceived adulthood and age are dynamic and fluid. For instance, during the months that are closer to people's birthdays, the more likely people will feel like their chronological age. During the months that are farther from their birthdays, people are more likely not feel younger or older.

SANDWICH GENERATION

In adulthood, many people fall into the **sandwich generation**. This is the time period during which people have dependent children and are also taking care of their aging parents. Caretakers are typically women and many of them hold full-time jobs in the labor market. They are sandwiched between two dependent generations. They experience stress from this situation, which affects their own aging process. They may feel guilt about not helping their parents more, but then they also feel guilt about taking resources from their children in order to care for their parents. The time commitment and financial burden are sometimes enormous. Prior research suggests that around 30 percent of women belong to the sandwich generation, where they are offering monetary or direct assistance to their parents as well as providing care for their own children (Pierret 2006).

OLD AGE

A traditional marker of **old age** is 65 years. Nearly 14 percent of the U.S. population is 65 or older and the percentage has been steadily increasing over the last 100 years. The U.S. Census predicts that this portion of the population will increase to 19 percent by 2030 because of the baby boomers (Vincent and Velkoff 2010), a group of people born between 1946 and 1964.

"Well, maybe I'd like to have eternal rest, too, did you ever think of that?"

© 2014 Cartoonresource. Used under license of Shutterstock, Inc.

thinking *critically*

In the United States, a little over 50 percent of this older population has not made any plans for a cemetery plot or cremation services (Quadagno 2011). More than 66 percent of them have not made a will or trust. More than 75 percent of them have not made any funeral arrangements in advance. It is sometimes difficult for Americans to discuss death. This means that children, friends, or government agencies will have to manage these activities, and typically be forced to make the decisions in a short amount of time right after the person passes away and during a very emotional period in their lives—losing a loved one. The aging population will also decrease the amount of money going to income taxes and consequently put a strain on social services that are reliant on tax revenue. One in particular is Social Security. As the ratio of worker to retired person changes, there is less money going into Social Security and more money going out in benefits, which threatens its solvency. Many scholars and policymakers are debating the best solution for this problem. They discuss raising the age at which people can receive Social Security benefits, decreasing the amount of benefits, basing the benefits off of need rather than solely age, or shuffling the responsibility off to private businesses. Conversely, an increase in this older population means that certain industries in the economy will benefit, from health care services to pharmaceutical companies. Advancements in these industries will have positive effects for future generations. Because of their needs, the 65-year-olds and older population will also create jobs for the younger generations who may gain employment as service workers in a number of industries that directly and indirectly assist the needs of the older population. Finally, as people live longer, their relationships last longer. For instance, more grandchildren will have more time to spend with their grandparents and, in many ways, the resulting effects will be socially positive.

SUMMARY

Everyone ages. But we do not all age in the same way. Some may focus on their chronological age, while others evaluate aging based on functionality. Others find that their social roles influence their aging processes and change their subjective age identities. A large number of theories on aging have emerged over the last century, ranging from micro theories (e.g., disengagement and activity theories) to mezzo theories (e.g., exchange theory and social constructionism) to macro theories (e.g., age integration theory and critical gerontology theory). The discipline of biology also offers a number of theories to explain how the body weakens over time. The life course perspective, however, encompasses all theoretical levels and implies that actions taken now will have lasting consequences over many life stages. One important life stage is transitioning into adulthood, which typically occurs between the ages of 18 and 30. People between the ages of 40 and 55, usually women, are often a part of the sandwich generation, where they are taking care of their aging parents while simultaneously taking care of their children. Old age is commonly considered to begin at age 65. This older population is growing and will predictably reach 19 percent of the U.S. population by 2030. That demographic change will have a number of positive and negative effects on society.

Suggested Reading:

Shanahan, Michael J., Erik J. Porfeli, Jeylan T. Mortimer, and Lance D. Erickson. 2005. "Subjective Age Identity and the Transition to Adulthood: When Do Adolescents Become Adults?" Pp. 225-255 in *On the Frontier of Adulthood: Theory, Research, and Public Policy*, edited by Richard A. Settersten, Jr., Frank K. Furstenberg Jr., and Ruben C. Rumbaut. Chicago, IL: The University of Chicago Press.

ACTIVE LEARNING PROJECTS

In Class:

1. Pretend that you work for an organization that educates people about the characteristics and needs of the aging population. Create a flyer with pertinent information on it that the organization could give out to community members.
2. Write about an experience that you feel represents a time when you realized you were transitioning out of adolescence.

---

3. Watch parts of the movie *The Curious Case of Benjamin Button* and, in a small group, decide how it exemplifies the life course perspective.
4. Imagine that you woke up tomorrow as a person over 65 years old. In a small group, list some ways that life would be better and worse than it is now.
5. In a small group, list some jokes that involve older people and discuss the features that make the jokes supposedly funny and why.

Out of Class:

1. Read the book *Tuesdays with Morrie* and identify the four categories of aging: chronological, functional, social roles, and subjective.
2. Go online and fill out a free living will document. In an essay, discuss its positive and negative points without sharing any sensitive information.
3. Write a letter to a loved one who has passed away, saying the things that you wish you could have said while that person was still alive.
4. Do an hour of community service for an assisted living center and write an essay about your experience and what you learned.
5. Go to Google Images on the Internet and type in "magazine covers" and estimate the percentage of the covers that show different age groups (e.g., 0–17, 18–30, 31–64, and 65+) and identify how the different age groups are portrayed. Write an essay regarding why this might be and what effect, if any, it has on the perceptions of people who read the magazines.

KEY TERMS

Activity theory	Emerging adulthood	Old age
Age integration theory	Exchange theory	Sandwich generation
Aging	Functional aging	Social constructionism
Biology theories of aging	Life course perspective	Social roles and aging
Chronological aging	Macro theories of aging	Subjective aging
Critical gerontology approach	Mezzo theories of aging	Transition to adulthood
Disengagement theory	Micro theories of aging	

PART IV

How Do Sociologists Explain Human Similarities and Differences?

chapter 8

Social Groups, Structures, and Institutions

KEEP IN MIND

- A group consists of two or more people who share similar cultural traits, participate in similar social practices, and have a feeling of affinity for one another.
- A social structure refers to a set of interrelated social statuses that have identifiable social roles and reflects a pattern of social behavior over time.
- A social institution consists of social structures and cultural ideologies, and arises to solve a societal problem.

BE ABLE TO: See the interconnected social statuses and roles of the social structures and institutions in which you live and work.

SOCIAL GROUPS

When we observe the people around us, it is easy to see that some people look similar to us in some ways and that other people look different from us. These similarities and differences may be found in clothing or other material items, in ideology and language use, or in body appearance and movement. Sometimes we consciously try to look similar or different from other people and at other times it happens without us consciously recognizing it. One of the reasons we are simultaneously similar and different from other people is because we live in groups, typically multiple groups with differing characteristics. A **group** consists of two or more people who share similar cultural traits, participate in similar social practices, and have a feeling of affinity for one another. Groups can exhibit great variation. They vary in type, membership size, activity, closeness, goals, and geographical proximity, among other characteristics. With this amount of variation, some scholars prefer to define groups with narrower standards, such as the members needing to be familiar with each other, while other scholars accept a comparatively open definition, where the members need not even be in the same nation let alone know one another. In the latter case, a group is similar to an aggregate or category. An **aggregate** refers to a collection of people who are in the same place at the same time, such as people at a theme park or on the beach, and a **category** refers to a collection of people who share some characteristic, such as being college educated. People may move in and out of aggregates, categories, and groups—that is, the labels may change when they change their behavior. For example, some people on the beach may begin to interact (e.g., build sand castles together or have lunch together) and then move from individuals in the aggregate to members of a group. Or, people who fall under the same ethnic characteristic but live in different countries may begin to participate online in response to a particular protest, moving them from a category of people who share an ethnic characteristic to a group of people. After the protest, however, they may end their online participation and go back to being a category of people who share an ethnicity. Some examples of groups include families, clubs, social movements, businesses, nations, and multinational organizations.

For sociologists, group membership is a key component to understanding human behavior. Sociologists assume that in order for people to survive over time they either have lived with a group of people for an extended period of time or they currently live within a group. Even a hermit would have had to be part of a group at some point, such as during childhood, and this group membership in many ways continues to shape his or her thoughts and behaviors. Moreover, sociologists assume that groups are what Durkheim called *sui generis*. They have unique qualities of their own, above and beyond the individual characteristics of their members. That is, group attributes influence individual group members at the same time that individual group members influence the constitution of the group. One example of this is when family members invoke the family's surname to prod other family members to do something or stop doing something: "Johnsons never give up!" Or, another example comes from sports. In some cases, the reason that a team won a championship cannot be explained by the talents of each player, but rather by the combination of players together. The logical conclusion is that people may have innate characteristics and individual psychological tendencies, but they are also powerfully affected by the group within which they reside.

CHECK POINT: What is the difference between a group, an aggregate, and a category?

Primary and Secondary Groups

Groups may be divided into two broad categories: primary groups and secondary groups. **Primary groups** tend to be comparatively small in size, and the group members have long-lasting and intimate ties with one another. This type of group exacts strong emotional and physical demands on its members and the borders of the group are relatively closed for entering and exiting. Some examples of primary groups include marriages, families, sports teams, church congregations, military units, and street gangs. Not all of these examples are always primary groups. Not all sports teams and not all church congregations, for example, would qualify as primary groups. Yet, many would. Charles Horton Cooley

coined the term *primary group* and argued that this type of group is particularly powerful in shaping a person's socialization experiences. Group members quickly learn the cultural values, norms, beliefs, and practices of the group and are compelled to follow along. They experience significant social control. The primary group also affects the group members' interpretations of the society's broader cultural traditions. In some cases, the primary group's culture may align with the society's culture and, in other cases, it may not, such as the New York Fire Department versus the Ku Klux Klan.

The family, however, is one of the most powerful primary groups. Although the definition of the family is controversial, sociologists often classify a group as a **family** when the relationships are based on marriage, blood, or adoption; when there are expressive and instrumental characteristics present, such as experiencing love and shelter; and when the members hold a sense of unity with one another. The family is typically the first group that begins to socialize an individual from birth. It acculturates the individual and sets a foundation for his or her social and economic progress. Evidence indicates that even the

timing of entrance into this primary group has lifetime effects. That is, birth order matters because different resources and behaviors accompany different time periods when the children are born. Therefore, when a child is the first-born, he or she is likely to have a different personality than a middle born or last born, independent of biology (Leman 2009). The composition of the family, however, has changed in the last 50 years. The percentage of married couples who have children under 18 years of age has gone from around 40 percent to 22 percent, while the percentage of children born to unmarried women has risen to 41 percent (Martin et al. 2012). How the family affects people, therefore, is predicted to change as well.

"It helps to be thick skinned around here."

Secondary groups consist of relatively impersonal ties between group members that are typically more formal in nature and organized to accomplish a particular objective.

Workplaces often house secondary groups, where the workers have relationships but less social intimacy and they are attempting to achieve a formal goal. The relationships are consequently more instrumental than emotional. Secondary groups, however, do have the potential to facilitate or even transform into primary groups, under certain circumstances, such as coworkers who date and marry or gangs that take on family-like qualities.

CHECK POINT: How might groups in which people are *not* members affect them?

In-groups and Out-groups

While group membership has a significant effect on people, groups in which people are not members also have a considerable impact on them. These outcomes may occur indirectly, such as in the way that the civil rights movement influenced people who were not a part of the movement. Or, they may have a direct effect, as when charity groups offer assistance to persons in need. Sociologists, therefore, distinguish between in-groups and out-groups. An **in-group** is the group of which a person is a member. An **out-group** is the group of which a person is not a member. Colloquially, we make this distinction quite frequently when we say "us" and "them." In-groups clearly influence the social identity of group members. Yet, out-groups may have an impact on the social identity of other group members as well. During high school, many groups emerge, from jocks to skaters, and members from each group develop a sense of what the out-group members think of them. In some cases, this knowledge may result in physically violent interactions and, in other cases, the impact may be more emotional.

Reference Groups

Since group members are aware of other groups, a reference group is another important concept. A **reference group** is the group that is used as the standard of evaluation. When people want to emulate a group's cultural attributes, it is a positive reference group. Many people consider firefighters to be heroes and judge their own qualities based on the qualities they perceive firefighters to have. When people reject a group's cultural attributes, it is a negative reference group. Some individuals estimate the costs of gang membership. Both types of reference groups are used to help people determine what they prefer and how they want to be and to what extent that they believe they are currently acceptable or not. Such criteria of evaluation may include physical attractiveness or ability, intellectual prowess, knowledge of certain things, level of spirituality, or willingness to take a stand for something. After the evaluation and comparison of themselves with the positive or negative reference group, people may experience a range of emotions, from pride and satisfaction to depression and unworthiness. The validity of their evaluation may be incorrect, but still effective nonetheless.

FORMAL ORGANIZATIONS AND BUREAUCRACIES

Over time, societies have advanced technologically and economically, leading to very large and complex secondary groups called formal organizations. **Formal organizations** are intentionally designed entities that have an official system of operation for the purpose of achieving an overt objective. These include government agencies, economic corporations, health care facilities, educational institutions, and public unions, among others. Today, formal organizations are highly interwoven with each other to the point that when one formal organization encounters problems, other formal organizations experience the ripple effect. In response, the government has created new formal organizations, such as the Securities and Exchange Commission (SEC), to monitor and regulate other formal organizations. Since formal organizations attempt to meet the diverse needs of a complex society, almost all of the country's jobs come from formal organizations.

Given that formal organizations are created to accomplish a specific goal and that they reside in a marketplace of competition under the scrutiny of other formal organizations, they attempt to be as efficient as possible. This means that they standardize their operations and policies. The result is that many of them become bureaucracies. **Bureaucracies** are formal organizations that have hierarchal structures with specific lines of authority and overt rules and procedures for how to carry out daily tasks. Many people have complained that bureaucracies are inefficient, creating bureaucratic red tape. Consequently, bureaucracy has come to represent wastefulness and ineffectiveness in popular conversation. However, due to the complexity of the modern world, especially as it has globalized over the last 50 years, bureaucracies have actually facilitated great advancements across society, from domestic and international government institutions to domestic and international charities. New technologies, medications, disaster relief efforts, security procedures, energy systems, trading units, educational advancements, media activities, and many other things have emerged quickly and proficiently relative to historical social progress because of bureaucracies. Yet, despite the stunning innovations and improvements that can be credited to bureaucracies, Max Weber warned us over a 100 years ago of their potential negative effects. He said that bureaucracies could become like an iron cage, limiting individual freedoms and dehumanizing society so that humans are no more than machine parts. Considering the number of regulations in the government and in large businesses, his fears have arguably come to fruition in many ways.

CHECK POINT: What are bureaucracies?

Social Structure

In large part, what makes a bureaucracy distinct is its formalized social structure. In sociology, **social structure** is a broad term, but in this case refers to a set of interrelated social statuses that have identifiable social roles, which result in patterned behavior over time. A **social status** is the position that a person holds within the structure, and a **social role** is the behavior that the social status is expected or prescribed to do. In the classroom, someone is the instructor and someone else is the student. Both have a relationship to each other and so they know what is expected of them. Patterns of behavior consequently emerge. Traditionally, the instructor stands in front of the classroom speaking and the students sit in chairs listening. Moreover, because of this social structure, both instructor and students can predict the future. If it is a semester system, they know where each of them will be in four months, down to the day and even the time of day. They will both be in the classroom giving and taking a final exam. This knowledge is possible because the education system has a stable social structure. There are statuses: president, provost, deans, administration staff, professors, and students. Each has a role to play on certain timetables.

A broader definition of social structure would not focus on the formalized connection between statuses but rather on the distributions of the social statuses in relation to one another. For example, because of past and current birth and death rates, demographers are able to describe the age and gender structure of the United States. They are then able to predict a pattern of growth over the next several decades where by 2030 people aged 65 or older will constitute 19 percent of the U.S. population. This type of forecasting allows lawmakers to prepare for a new social environment and the resulting consequences, such as potential pressures on government benefits.

Social structures consequently constrain our behavior. They are very difficult to change and so people typically maneuver within them. For example, if a college student had a complaint about a professor, the student would not be able to go directly to the president of the university. There are other social statuses to go through first that have a specific role for such situations. Perhaps, the student would speak with the chair of the department, then the ombudsman, and then possibly the dean. A pathway through the social structure would need to be followed. Similarly, there is a pathway for graduating from college. A student is typically not able to construct his or her own major. Rather, the student must choose a major from a set number of majors and then follow the pathway to obtain that major by taking certain required courses and choosing from a limited number of elective courses to fulfill a defined number of college credits. Consequently, students are forced to take specific courses, interact with particular professors, pay a determined amount of money, and graduate within an allotted time frame, regardless of what the students consider to be right or wrong. Metaphorically, social structures are a social maze that everyone is required to navigate.

MASTER STATUS AND STATUS INCONSISTENCY

In a complex society, everyone holds several statuses and performs many roles at the same time. A man may be a father, spouse, teacher, worker, friend, child, and volunteer, simultaneously. Yet, one status may overshadow all of the other statuses. A **master status** is the social status that dominates all of the others in the individual's mind or the minds of other people and through which the person will be evaluated in terms of what role he or she is supposed to play. For example, a person may be a fabulous auto mechanic, a star poker player, and a recently open homosexual male. The social status through which he may see himself most often and through which most other people may see him is as a homosexual male. The result is that people who did not know his sexual orientation before but found out recently will likely change their behavior with him, for better or worse. Other master statuses may

"Don't worry, Skeeter, the Big Guy is really gonna take to you."

include racial identity, gender identity, religious affiliation, political party affiliation, and even a hobby, such as a mountain climber. We see signs of a master status even at the social structural level. On college campuses, it is often said without thought that there is a "basketball" game tonight and then tomorrow night there is a "women's basketball" game. The master status, however, may change depending on the social context and over time.

Status inconsistency refers to the idea that a person holds two or more social statuses that are at odds with each other based on social expectations. A female dentist or a male hygienist are examples. Often status inconsistency occurs when the **achieved status**, a position someone has worked for, is in conflict with an **ascribed status**, a position someone has been given by society. A person may have achieved the status of dentist but also been ascribed the status of female by society and patients may not be used to this combination of statuses. There is nothing inherently incompatible with the combination of statuses. Rather, it is the role expectations of the social statuses that result in the idea of inconsistency.

ROLE CONFLICT AND ROLE STRAIN

Due to the overlapping social structures in our lives, role conflict may occur. **Role conflict** represents the situation where a person holds two or more social statuses that have corresponding roles that are socially incompatible. An example is a person who works in the financial industry and wants to give a friend some valuable information regarding future stock trades with a specific company. This person has a work role and the role of a friend. However, by sharing this valuable information, he or she may be taking part in insider trading—which has legal ramifications. On the less dramatic side, another example is when a married parent wants to spend time alone with a spouse. The person is a parent and a spouse, but in many instances he or she

"I work outside the home, inside the home, and occasionally on top of the home."

© 2043 Cartoonresource. Used under license of Shutterstock, Inc.

cannot fulfill the roles of both statuses at the same time. The needs of the children may take precedence over other desires and obligations. **Role strain** reflects the idea that some social statuses have very demanding roles. A parent likely experiences role strain quite frequently. The parent must not only play the role of mother or father but also the roles of chef, shopper, doctor, teacher, psychologist, entertainer, and maid, to name a few. Attempting to fulfill all of these different roles for that one status can be very tiring. But the social structure, in this case of the family, demands it.

thinking *critically*

To what extent is it reasonable to complain that someone has it easier or harder by tallying up and comparing roles?

JOB SKILLS: Avoiding Job Burnout

Of all of the developed countries in the world, the United States has the least amount of vacation. It is not surprising, therefore, that approximately 77 percent of workers complain about job burnout (Lorenz 2009). They feel so much stress from their jobs that they consider quitting. Some feel overwhelmed with the position itself and others experience a conflict between work and family life. As an employee, you may consider the concepts of role strain and role conflict. Identify the number of roles that your work position is supposed to fulfill and to what extent they conflict with non-work-related roles. Consciously examining and understanding these dimensions of your job may provide valuable information to use with your employer to change the situation before job burnout occurs, such as receiving a promotion, increase in pay, more time off, a different work schedule, an assistant, or something else. As an employer, considering the extent to which employees are experiencing role strain and role conflict may assist in developing strategies to keep employee moral up and employee productivity strong.

SOCIAL INSTITUTIONS

Social institutions consist of social structures that have common cultural values and norms for different statuses and roles, all with the purpose of solving a societal problem. They are less structured than formal organizations. But they are also larger and reach across a broader range of society. In terms of solving societal problems, social institutions bring new members into society, educate new members, keep members safe and orderly, keep members informed of new events, feed members, give members something to do, and deal with members who die. Social institutions include the health care system, the education system, the criminal justice system, the mass media, and the economic system. Each social institution has a network of formal organizations within it and an overriding cultural ideology. For example, the health care system emerged to help newborns, the sick, and the dying. But the government did not plan and build up each formal organization. They grew together organically. At the same time, there is a general cultural ideology of assisting people with their medical needs first and letting other social institutions worry about the financial costs. Social institutions do change, but they change very slowly. One reason is because they are also interconnected with other social institutions in society. For example, the economy is connected to the government and both are connected to the media. Due to the combination of different and interconnected social institutions, societies are able to progress over time.

SUMMARY

In every society, some people appear and act similarly in some ways while others appear and act differently. One of the reasons is that everyone belongs to a variety of groups, which consist of two or more people who share cultural traits and do the same social practices. Two important groups are the primary group and the secondary group. The primary group consists of close network ties and demands conformity. It is also usually the group that has the most impact on socializing people. The secondary group consists of instrumental ties. The group is together to accomplish a task. Formal organizations are made of secondary groups. When they have defined hierarchal lines of authority and objective rules to follow, they become bureaucracies. All groups, including primary and secondary, or formal organizations and bureaucracies, consist of social structures. Social structures are a network of social statuses and roles. Social institutions incorporate social structures but also have a general cultural ideology and organically emerge to solve the society's problems.

Suggested Reading:

Stempel, Carl. 2006. "Gender, Social Class, and the Sporting Capital-Economic Capital Nexus." *Sociology of Sport Journal* 23:273-292.

ACTIVE LEARNING PROJECTS

In Class:

1. Write about the imagined reactions you would get if you treated coworkers like family and family like coworkers.
2. Identify a positive reference group and write what you like about that group and why?
3. Watch the video *True Colors*, which was produced by Diane Sawyer in the 1990s, and discuss how it exemplifies the concepts of category, in-groups/out-groups, master status, ascribed status, and role conflict.
4. In a small group, identify your master status and discuss why it is that status and not something else.
5. In a small group, discuss the costs and benefits of being in the primary and secondary groups in which you are a member.

Out of Class:

1. Identify the person you think has the greatest amount of role strain and write this person an appreciative letter.
2. Watch several TV shows or YouTube.com videos and identify examples of status inconsistency.
3. Draw a map of the connections between the social statuses of a social structure that you are involved in, such as your family or school, and list out each status's role expectations. Also, pinpoint your location in that social structure and discuss why you are at that point.
4. Write an essay on which master status you think is the most influential socially and psychologically in the United States (e.g., gay/lesbian, upper class, felon, religious).
5. Identify your in-groups and out-groups during high school and write a reflection paper on why those were your in-groups and out-groups.

KEY TERMS

Achieved status	Group	Role strain
Aggregate	In-group	Secondary group
Ascribed status	Master status	Social institution
Bureaucracy	Out-group	Social role
Category	Primary group	Social status
Family	Reference group	Social structure
Formal organization	Role conflict	Status inconsistency

chapter 9

Social Stratification, Inequality, and Class

KEEP IN MIND

- Social stratification refers to the idea that groups and categories of people are ranked in a hierarchal system where they are allocated different types and amounts of resources.
- Social inequality represents the reality that in a stratification system everyone does not receive equal types and amounts of resources.
- There are two types of social inequality: inequality of condition and inequality of opportunity.
- Class is an important dimension of social stratification and inequality.
- In the United States, approximately 15 percent of the population falls under the poverty line.
- Higher education is significantly associated with greater upward social mobility.

BE ABLE TO: Think critically about why people are in their social class positions.

SOCIAL STRATIFICATION

In every society as far back as recorded history informs us, there has been a degree of social stratification. **Social stratification** refers to the idea that groups and categories of people are ranked in a hierarchal system where they are allocated certain types and amounts of resources. Depending on the individual's membership in a group or category, he or she will experience more or less of what the society has to offer. Resources are finite, meaning that they are limited in number, as with the limited availability of housing. But complex societies like the United States have an enormous range of resources, from the basic needs of food, clothing, and shelter, to the intangible assets of prestige, power, and

freedom. Social stratification is apparent even in smaller units. Among the 50 states, one of the highest paid employees is often a football or basketball coach (Fischer-Baum 2013). At the university level, we also see resources and prestige allocated differently by sports teams. Football and basketball tend to enjoy more resources than do swimming and soccer. Down to the family unit, there is evidence that women put in more hours of unpaid domestic labor than do men, even when both of them work in the paid labor force. When men do put in a similar number of hours they are allocated the tasks that are comparatively less mentally and emotionally draining (Futrelle 2012).

What this indicates is that social stratification also represents **social inequality**. Some groups, such as sports teams, and some categories of people, such as men, experience an unequal share of desirable resources. There are two general types of social inequality—inequality of condition and inequality of opportunity. People differ in terms of their material conditions or comforts and they differ in terms of their opportunities to obtain advantageous goods and services. For example, we might wonder if the system of writing recommendation letters for college and for an occupational position is fair. It arguably is not fair. People who have letter writers that are in positions of power or who are well known are likely to have their letters weighted more heavily in their favor than someone else who is equally competent but without the same personal connections. One person has more opportunity for success and therefore a greater likelihood of experiencing advantageous social conditions. At the same time, the person who has more respected letter writers likely already comes from advantageous social conditions. Importantly, as the sociologist Martin Marger (2008) notes, very little of the inequality we see between groups and categories of people is a result of shared differences in innate drive or psychological ambition but is rather a consequence of a stratified social system. It is therefore predictable who will have the highest likelihood of enjoying certain resources based on group membership or affiliation with a particular social category.

JOB SKILLS: Recognizing Stratification

Businesses in the United States tend to be structured in a social hierarchy that resembles a triangle—a few positions at the top and more positions toward the bottom. Some employees become frustrated or upset with their superiors. Yet, the employee who understands the stratification system is able to realize that in many ways it is the position that matters more than the individual. Bosses may come and go but the requirements of the position will remain the same and consequently put similar pressures on anyone who fills that position. In her book *Men and Women of the Corporation*, Rosabeth Moss Kanter (1993) discovered that male secretaries behaved similarly as female secretaries. She also found that the number of particular employees, such as males versus females or Whites versus Blacks, made a difference in people's attitudes and behaviors. Consequently, for example, if the boss is one of a few females in the office and her superiors are males she may act differently than if the gender ratio were more balanced. Recognizing these stratification characteristics—the business structure and employee demographics—may help with office relations.

Party, Status, and Class

Max Weber defined three general dimensions of social stratification and inequality: party, status, and class. With the concept of **party**, Weber argued that people band together to achieve a particular resource. Parties may be political or they may be clubs or unions or some other voluntary association. The main point, however, is that they are differentiated by **power**, which is the ability to act despite opposition from others. Some parties have more power than other parties. They range in social influence and domination. For example, some groups promote abortion rights for women while other groups strive to restrict these rights or promote the rights of fetuses. A moral war occurs as parties organize staff to win over more people in the society to support their ideas. Along these lines, many groups of people are stratified by power. Some religious groups have more ability to promote their values than other religious groups. Some charities have more access to funding and media sources than other charities. At the university level, some fraternities and sororities likely have more social influence than others in the Greek system. People therefore also experience inequality with respect to power.

In terms of **status**, Weber focused on the status positions of large numbers of people within the society and the relative honor or prestige that the status positions held in the stratified system. Sociologist Lauren Rivera (2010) used Weber's ideas to identify consequential status distinctions when she studied an exclusive nightclub in a major northeastern metropolitan area. Not everyone had the same opportunity to get into the nightclub because the doormen made exclusionary decisions based on status. Women were more likely to be allowed in because they were perceived as comparatively less likely to cause disruptions and because they were perceived to increase alcohol sales, as men bought them drinks in order to talk to them. African Americans and other racial minorities had a harder time gaining entrance into the nightclub because their status reflected less wealth in the minds of the doormen. Although places like nightclubs are primarily entertainment venues, they are also places to build social networks, from potential marriage partners to business partners. Entrance or exclusion based on status can consequently mean more than enjoying or missing out on a night of fun. Occupations are also ranked by prestige in society. Physicians experience more prestige than nurses, for example. Some of the rewards appear not only in salary but also in social settings. Status distinctions therefore have a diverse set of consequences that result in social inequality.

For Weber, **class** refers to the similarities among people with respect to their opportunities to achieve economic advancement. In the United States, there are a number of ways to categorize class. One way is: underclass, working poor, working class, lower middle class, middle-middle class, upper-middle class, and upper class. A primary component of this conception is money. There is great variation in terms of people's income and wealth in the United States. **Income** is the amount of money people make from salaries and wages and any earnings from investments. **Wealth** is the totality of economic assets that someone owns, minus any debts. Although a person cannot have a negative income, they can have negative wealth. All of their possessions may be worth less than all of their debts. In 2012, for example, approximately 30 percent of homeowners owed more in loans on their home than their houses were currently worth on the housing market, meaning that they secured a mortgage to buy a house and then the house decreased in value enough to be lower than the loan amount (Christie 2012). New college graduates may experience negative wealth because their student loans may be larger than the economic worth of all of their possessions.

Most Americans tend to believe that the income and wealth distributions in the United States resemble a diamond—a small percentage of rich people at the top, most people in the middle, and a small percentage of poor people at the bottom. However, in reality, this distribution looks more like a tear drop—most people relegated to the bottom. If we change the perspective and examine the percentage of income and wealth that the wealthiest hold compared to the percentage that the poorest hold, the picture looks more like a sledge hammer. The wealthiest hold the majority of the money in the United States. In 2011, the Census reports that the top 20 percent of income earners by household—the households that made

the most money in the year—garnered 51.1 percent of all U.S. income. In order words, 80 percent of households shared 49 percent of the total income. Most of the money is at the very top. The top 5 percent of income earning households enjoyed 22 percent of the total income, while the lowest 20 percent of income earning households made only 3.2 percent of the total income in the United States. The level of stratification and inequality is even more dramatic by wealth. Sociologist G. William Domhoff (2013) reports that the average amount of wealth held by the top 1 percent of wealthiest Americans is about $16.5 million while the bottom 40 percent have no wealth at all. Rather, they are in debt for about $10.5 thousand, on average. The top 1 percent hold about 34 percent of all the wealth in the United States, and the next 19 percent hold 47.5 percent, totaling 81.5 percent of U.S. wealth for the top 20 percent. That leaves the bottom 80 percent of Americans to share about 18.5 percent of the total wealth in the United States. Economic stratification and inequality in the United States is significant.

The Poor

In 2011, the U.S. poverty rate was 15 percent of the population (or, approximately 45 million people). The poverty rate is based on poverty thresholds, which are defined by specific dollar amounts for different sizes of family units, ranging from one person to nine or more persons. If a family of a certain size makes less money in a year than the threshold number they are considered to be in poverty. For example, the Census reports that the weighted average threshold for a family of four in 2011 was $23,021. Any family of four with a lower income than that number would be deemed officially poor. They determine these poverty thresholds based on a definition of **poverty** that was created in 1964 during President Lyndon Johnson's administration. They estimated how much a family of each unit size would spend on food in a year to eat a basic, nutritious diet and then they tripled that number to arrive at the poverty threshold. This idea assumes that families spend about one-third of their income on food. Although it is slightly more involved to calculate today's poverty thresholds, those are the fundamental definitions and processes that still determine who is poor in America and who is not.

t h i n k i n g *critically*

What are some potential criticisms of this definition of poverty? In other words, what is this definition not taking into consideration?

Both liberals and conservatives complain about this definition. Some liberals argue that it results in poverty thresholds that are too low because life has changed over the last 50 years. Due to globalization, food is comparatively cheaper than in the past while housing, health care, and education costs have risen substantially and are not included in the calculation. The definition also fails to consider cost of living by location. It is more expensive to live in an urban area than a rural area with respect to housing, health care, and education compared to the relatively minimal differences in food prices. Some conservatives argue that the definition leads to poverty thresholds that are too high because the poor are able to receive financial assistance in a wide range of areas, including food stamps, housing subsidies, health care, heating, electricity, and tax relief.

Although the demographic composition of the poor changes from year to year, depending on societal events, there are some important trends (DeNavas-Walt et al. 2012). In terms of numbers, the White population has the most people in poverty. However, the percentage of Whites in poverty is smaller than the percentages of other racial categories in poverty. Blacks or African Americans and Hispanics of any race both have over 25 percent of their populations living in poverty. More women are officially poor than men and 22 percent of all poor people are children, aged 17 or younger. The elderly who are aged 65 and older have the lowest percentage in poverty. The majority of the poor reside in city centers or metropolitan areas rather than in rural areas. Numerically, more Whites use public assistance and welfare than other racial groups, but Blacks or African Americans and Hispanics have higher within-group percentages than do Whites. Women and children also all have higher percentages than men and adults (Kim et al. 2012).

t h i n k i n g *critically*

Why are people poor?

Cultural and Structural Explanations of Poverty

Many theories attempt to explain the existence of poverty. A general categorical division pits cultural theories against structural theories. One of the popular cultural theories is called **culture of poverty** and it dates back to the 1940s. Its basic argument is that poor people have a different set of values, norms, beliefs, and social practices that are not necessarily immoral or wrong but that do not allow poor people to be economically competitive in modern times. For example, one of the cultural values may be to take life easy, to enjoy life, and one of the norms may be to not appear better than anyone else. Such values and

"I'd like to make $3.2 million a year, but I'll settle for $8 an hour

© 2014 Cartoonresource. Used under license of Shutterstock, Inc.

norms may hinder poor people from striving for good grades in school or from working extra hours on the job, resulting in fewer opportunities for gaining acceptance into top-tier colleges or finding well-paying employment and experiencing meaningful promotions. On the negative side, some argue that people in poverty learn to be dependent on others and on the government instead of being independent enough to move themselves out of poverty. Since culture is passed down through generations, the children of people in poverty also remain in poverty.

Currently, the majority of sociologists consider the culture of poverty argument to be flawed. The evidence appears to suggest that the culture of poverty thesis likely has the cause and effect relationship backwards. That is, rather than culture causing poverty, poverty seems to be causing culture. Moreover, other researchers find that a significant percentage of people in poverty actually hold the same mainstream cultural values, norms, and beliefs as typical middle-class individuals, such as wanting to gain an education, find a career, marry, own a home, have children, support the neighborhood and community, and be upstanding citizens. These results lead to the structural arguments. Decades ago two sociologists, Kingsley Davis and Wilbert Moore (1945), used the structural-functionalist perspective to explain that social stratification and inequality are necessary for the survival of the society. The basic ideas of their argument are that some social positions are less desirable but still important, such as waste removal managers, and some social positions require years of difficult training,

such as becoming a physician. These relatively time-intensive and intellectual positions are more critical for society, they argued. Someone needs to design a building first and then another person can construct the building. Society needs to fill all of the positions but it attaches greater rewards to the more difficult and critical ones to attract the most talented of the population. Therefore, the people who are in low-paying jobs are necessary for society but are compensated accordingly for the comparatively easier and fundamentally less critical work.

This functionalist perspective has fallen out of favor with current sociologists because the evidence does not support it. For instance, in the United States, sports athletes and entertainers make large sums of money. All of the top-paid actors in 2012 made over $10 million each. Yet, they are less critical to the survival of society than waste removal managers, elementary school teachers, or local law enforcement officers. Furthermore, the functionalist perspective assumes that the most talented reach their way to the top through hard work, a scenario that does not pan out for the majority of society. By inference, the top 1 percent of the wealthiest Americans would have earned their way up to this privileged position. However, if we broaden the perspective from focusing just on the United States to including all other nations, we would find that millions of Americans are part of the top 1 percent of people living in the world because it takes only $34,000 a year to be in the top 1 percent of global wage earners (Censky 2012). These Americans did not earn their way up to the top 1 percent of the world in terms of income. They were born into it. The U.S. social structure in relation to other nations facilitated their privileged position. Similarly in the United States, the majority of people in the upper classes inherit their wealthy positions (Marger 2008). Based on empirical evidence, social structure matters more than having a particular culture in terms of being in poverty or not.

Conflict theorists and world-system theorists expand on this explanation. The poor are in poverty as a result of the social systems of the particular country and the world, where the wealthy are able to draw resources from poor populations because they have control over powerful social institutions. Wealthy individuals are in positions of authority in the government, in the justice system, in the education system, in the military, in financial institutions, and in corporations. Consequently, they are able to design laws that favor themselves. In the United States, the vast majority of national political leaders come from the upper-middle and upper classes (Marger 2008). As an example of power, currently the majority of funding for public education comes from property taxes. The result is that if a child lives in a wealthy neighborhood, he or she is likely to go to a well-funded school that has up-to-date technology, marvelous material resources, an array of extracurricular activities, and teachers with quality educational training. The child who resides in a poor neighborhood does not experience these advantages. State governments could redistribute property tax funds equally across all school districts, yet such policy ideas are rejected because people in power would not benefit from such a change. Critics of the conflict perspective, however, highlight the fact that there are many wealthy people and groups that fight for the economic advancement of all classes, making it less of an us-versus-them situation, and that there are also a number of social programs that are specifically designed to help underprivileged categories of people.

SOCIAL MOBILITY

Throughout time, societies have operated with open and closed stratification systems. The concept of **open stratification systems** indicates that the social structure of the society has pathways that allow people to achieve desirable resources independent of their group affiliation or categorical status. The concept of **closed stratification systems** indicates that social structure limits a person's ability to achieve desirable resources because people are ascribed their social positions. Examples of closed systems include slavery, estate, and caste. In these systems, people are given an unchangeable status from birth and are consequently restricted from moving up or down the social and economic ladder. The United States and other Western countries operate under a stratification system that is comparatively open because they have stratification systems that are based on class. A class-based stratification system allows for a degree of **social mobility**, which refers to the process of moving through the stratification system. One way to measure social mobility is to calculate a person's or group's socioeconomic status (SES) at two different points in time. **Socioeconomic status** typically reflects similarities and differences by income and wealth, education, and occupation. Depending on their place along each dimension, people may be considered to belong to a similar class or not within the stratification system. For example, biomedical engineers make less money than physician assistants on average (Bureau of

Labor Statics 2012a), yet they likely have more education and occupational prestige. Consequently, they were arguably able to reach a higher class position in the stratification system than were physician assistants, despite earning less money.

There are four general types of social mobility. **Vertical mobility** represents movement up or down the stratification system. **Horizontal mobility** represents movement from one social position to another social position of the same rank. A person who quits his or her job

as a social worker and becomes a teacher is an example of horizontal mobility because the monetary compensation, years of education, and occupational prestige are similar between the two social positions. **Intragenerational mobility** reflects changes in social positions within a person's lifetime. A person who begins as a paralegal and becomes a lawyer experiences intragenerational mobility. **Intergenerational mobility** reflects changes in social positions across two or more lifetimes within the same family unit. A mother who is a nurse and has a daughter who becomes a doctor provides an example of intergenerational mobility. An individual and family may experience multiple types of social mobility.

Based on public opinion polls, the majority of Americans believe that social mobility is within their control and that there is a lot of upward social mobility in the United States. A particular favorite is the rags-to-riches story, where someone born in poverty is able to make it into the upper classes, typically through hard work. Unfortunately, the Brookings Institution, which is a nonprofit public policy organization, finds otherwise (Greenstone et al. 2013). The majority of Americans will remain in the social positions into which they were born, and most other Americans will move up or down only one rank, be it from working class to lower middle class, or from upper middle class down to middle-middle class. The current degree of social mobility in the United States is no greater than in other industrialized countries. Yet, higher education does remain a solid strategy of achieving upward social mobility in the United States, especially with respect to moving out of poverty. Greenstone and colleagues (2013) report that a person who earns a bachelor's degree is predicted to earn approximately twice as much income as someone who earns only a high school degree, equating to a difference of over $500,000 in earnings over the course of a lifetime.

SUMMARY

All societies have some degree of social stratification, which is the idea that different groups and categories of people are ranked in a social hierarchy. The result is that people experience social inequality, where some receive more or less of the society's desirable resources. Weber outlined three dimensions of modern stratification systems. Parties are groups that vie for power in society to accomplish a certain goal. Therefore, power is a stratification dimension. People are also ranked by status. Some statuses are given more rewards than other statuses. Class is the third stratification dimension. One of the main components of class is money. In the United States, there is great stratification and inequality by income and wealth. The top 20 percent of household income earners own about 51 percent of all

U.S. income while the wealthiest 20 percent control about 81 percent of all U.S. wealth. Approximately 15 percent of Americans live below the poverty level, which is based on food consumption patterns and family size. Scholars have explained the existence of poverty by highlighting the cultural characteristics of the poor and the structural factors of society. Most sociologists favor theoretical explanations that focus on social structure. The United States has a relatively open social stratification system, meaning that someone's ascribed status will not, by policy, limit his or her social mobility. Social mobility refers to the process of moving through the stratification system, either vertically or horizontally. Compared to other industrialized countries, the United States has an average amount of social mobility. Nonetheless, the one thing that has been shown to lead to great upward social mobility is attaining a higher education.

Suggested Reading:

Rivera, Lauren A. 2010. "Status Distinctions in Interaction: Social Selection and Exclusion at an Elite Nightclub." *Qualitative Sociology* 33:229-255.

ACTIVE LEARNING PROJECTS

In Class:

1. Make a list of dream jobs, a list of jobs you think you could get, and a list of jobs that you know you could get. What would it take to get hired in each job in terms of education, skills, and talent. Make a chart to record differences.
2. In a small group, list all of the expenses that a single person, a single mother with one child, and a married couple with two children would have in a month. Then, determine if a minimum wage salary would pay the bills, or what would be the minimum salary necessary.
3. Read sections of the book *Nickel and Dimed* by Barbara Ehrenreich and, in a small group, discuss the work ethic, ambition, and social structural constraints of the people in the book.
4. In a small group, make a poster that offers information on class inequality in the United States.
5. Think of some of the editorial cartoons that you've seen in newspapers, or look at some on Google Images. Try your hand at drawing one that you create out of your own imagination about class inequality in the United States.

Out of Class:

1. Look up your county on the U.S. Census website and determine the percentage of people who are in poverty and the demographic distribution—race, gender, age, etc.
2. Go back in your family history and identify the jobs that each person had, in order to get a sense of your family's intergenerational mobility.
3. Volunteer for a food bank or some other organization that works with the economically disadvantaged and write about your experience.
4. Research the history and beliefs of a social movement that relates to class inequality (e.g., labor movement or Occupy Wall Street) and write a report on it, offering ideas about the effects it may have had on society and on individuals.
5. Interview a server at an expensive restaurant and at an inexpensive restaurant, detailing any similarities and differences about their jobs, perspectives, patrons, and anything else. Then, write a report on your findings.

KEY TERMS

Class	Intragenerational mobility	Social mobility
Closed stratification systems	Open stratification systems	Social stratification
Culture of poverty	Party	Socioeconomic status
Horizontal mobility	Poverty	Status
Income	Power	Vertical mobility
Intergenerational mobility	Social inequality	Wealth

chapter **10**

Racial and Ethnic Inequality

- Race is defined as a set of socially constructed categories into which people place themselves and others based on perceived biological distinctions, while ethnicity is a set of categories based on perceived cultural traits.
- The concepts of between-group variation and within-group variation help explain why race is a social construction and not inherently biological.
- The concept of racial formations represents the idea that powerful institutions and groups negotiate which racial categories will be available for people to identify with.
- There are different explanations for the socioeconomic gap between Whites and minorities depending on the target minority group.
- Racism consists of prejudicial attitudes and discriminatory actions toward a racial category or categories of people.

BE ABLE TO: Explain why race is a social construction and not objectively biological.

E ven before the signing of the Declaration of Independence, race and ethnicity have proven to be important social categories. **Race** is defined as a set of socially constructed categories into which people place themselves and others based on perceived biological distinctions. That is, according to sociologists, a person's race is not inherently biological but rather a manifestation of what the person and society believe his or her race to be, making it inherently social. **Ethnicity** is a set of socially constructed categories into which people place themselves and others based on perceived cultural traits. Ethnicity, therefore, is also social rather than biological. As a result, both race and ethnicity become powerful dimensions of the social stratification system in the United States. Depending on a person's race and ethnicity, he or she experiences more or less of what society has to offer.

RACE, BIOLOGY, AND SOCIAL THINKING

For many Americans, the idea that race is not inherently biological would seem odd. Given the country's level of racial diversity, Americans interact frequently with a variety of racial and ethnic groups. There are people who look White, Black, Asian, and Native American, for example. In theory, because there is variation in skin pigmentation and other facial features, such as eye shape and hair texture, there are different racial categories. In this case, race would be inherently biological and the social part would only be in the naming of the categories.

However, today's intense focus on the outward distinctions of skin color and facial features in the effort to categorize people into a certain race has not always been the case. Especially after Charles Darwin published his extremely influential book, *The Origin of Species*, in 1859, many people in the United States began to hypothesize that racial groups differed by something inside the body. That is, they considered the idea that different collections of people may actually have been different "races" or species. Some intellectuals in the late 19th and early 20th centuries attempted to determine whether non-Whites were physically different than Whites in some way, be it a different organ, muscle, or bone structure. Many U.S. states in the early 1900s also adopted a one-drop rule, which meant that if a person had "a drop of Negro blood" (often technically stated as 1/16 or 1/32 of Negro blood, which was identified through hypodescent or lineage) that person would be considered Black. As a side note, this definition did not pass legislation for many years before 1900 because so many people who were considered White had come from ancestral lines that intermixed with Blacks due to slavery. In other words, a large population of multiracial people did not want to lose the privileges of being labeled White, even though their skin tones were clearly White. The law of hypodescent, or the one-drop rule, officially ended in all U.S. states in the early 1980s, but the abstract idea of it to separate Whites from minority groups remains culturally in use today. Nonetheless, after all of the scientific attempts to find something internally distinctive between different racial groups, nothing was found. All racial groups had the same internal organs, muscle and bone structures, hormones, DNA, and a host of other anatomical and physiological features. These findings are logical because members of all racial groups originate from the same species, Homo sapiens.

Yet, even in the current time period, we still hear rumblings that some racial groups must be biologically different because its members are so prevalent in—and excel at—a certain sport. For example, Kenyans often dominate long-distance running. One explanation is that they are genetically different in a way that makes them better at that type of running (Finn et al. 2013). This argument is not a problem. Yet, some people then extrapolate from this statement to use Kenyans

© 2014 KatarinaF. Used under license of Shutterstock, Inc.

as evidence that Blacks are naturally better runners. What is typically not considered is that Kenyans do not dominate the short-distance races, and we do not see Blacks from other countries, including many other countries in Africa, competing at the same level as the Kenyans in the long-distance races. What this indicates is that some people in the Black racial category are good at long-distance running and others are not, a situation which suggests that it is not the biological features of the racial category that makes a difference. Rather, Kenyans may indeed have some genetic advantage, not due to the color pigmentation of their skin or their racial category but rather due to their geography. People who have a generational history in that location have adapted to the physical environment, which in the case of the Kenyans may account for some of their ability to run long distances while also accounting for some of their inability to run short distances as competitively. Differences in geography, therefore, rather than racial identity accounts for the differences in sports ability. Notwithstanding the sports example, most people in the United States probably do not categorize people into different racial groups based on perceived biological differences within the body. Rather, it seems that the major way to categorize people by race today is by skin color.

RACE, SKIN COLOR, AND SOCIAL THINKING

Most Americans no longer focus on inward biological features to separate people into racial categories. Currently, most people focus primarily on skin color. One way to understand race as a social construction (i.e., created by humans) and not a process of objectively labeling biological reality is to use the concepts of between-group variation and within-group variation. **Between-group variation** measures the distance—or amount of differences—between two groups. **Within-group variation** measures the distance—or amount of differences—among members of the same group. If biology were the overriding factor in how people place themselves and others into different racial categories, we would expect to see a large difference in skin color between racial groups and a small difference in skin color within a racial group. Whites and Blacks, for example, should have a lot of difference between them in terms of skin color and all Whites should look relatively similar in terms of skin color and all Blacks should look relatively similar in terms of skin color. However, the evidence of skin color shows a great range of color tone for Whites (i.e., a large amount of within-group variation), going from very white to dark brown, such as seen with some Latinos and Arabs who often fall into the White racial category. Similarly, some Blacks have very dark skin while others actually have white skin. This means that there are millions of people who have the same skin color but are in different racial categories (i.e., a small amount of between-group variation). This outcome would not happen if our racial categories actually matched the biological reality of differing skin colors. People with the same skin color would be in the same racial category and not in different racial categories. Racial categorization, therefore, is a product of human perceptions of biology (e.g., skin color, hair texture, eye shape) rather than any objective labeling of biology.

Paleobiologist Nina Jablonski and research analyst George Chaplin (2000) studied the determining factors in skin color. They found that skin color is highly correlated with geographic latitude and UV radiation levels and that the gradation of skin color matches the range of latitudes and UV radiation exposure. In other words, the range in skin color is not blocked out in categories, such as White, Black, and Brown, but rather it is a continuum from darker to lighter depending on the human group's geographic location and level of exposure to UV rays. In our species' history and over many generations, groups that lived in areas where there was a lot of sun, such as the middle latitudes of Africa, China, and Latin America, adapted to the natural environment with dark skin. It was the body's way of protecting itself against sun damage and cancer. Individuals with lighter skin colors in those areas were less likely to live to adulthood and therefore less likely to reproduce and pass on their light skin color genes. Darker skin consequently spread through the population. However, as Homo sapiens migrated out of Africa, they moved into latitudes and climates with less sunlight. In appropriate doses, sunlight facilitates the development of vitamin D in the body and vitamin D helps with bone and brain development, among other benefits. Therefore, individuals in regions that had comparatively less sunlight needed lighter skin in order to allow the sun to facilitate the production of vitamin D. Lighter skin colored individuals were able to survive to adulthood and reproduce, spreading light skin tones across the population, since people with darker skin tones had a comparatively more difficult time producing adequate amounts of vitamin D and living to adulthood in those regions. In the end, this is how biologists explain the gradual change in skin color from the middle of Africa to the top of Norway, for example.

CHECK POINT: How does understanding between-group variation and within-group variation help explain race as a concept created by humans and race not as an objective labeling of biology?

RACE AS A SOCIAL CONSTRUCTION

Within our race categorization system, people have to negotiate their racial identity with others at the individual level and group level. In the early 1900s, individuals who were Jewish, Irish, and Italian were considered to be non-White. Over decades, and after economic progress, they were finally accepted as White, even though their skin color remained the same (Roediger 2005). In the 1940s, Gregory Howard Williams was born to a Black father who could pass as Italian and a White mother (Williams 1996). He grew up in Virginia until he was 10 years old. He thought that he was White and everyone considered him to be White based on skin color. Yet, after his parents divorced, he moved with his father to Indiana to be near family members. He learned that his father's side of the family identified as Black. He was suddenly considered to be Black too, and struggled with racial identification for years. After he reached adulthood he was more able to choose his racial identify for himself and he chose to remain identifying with being Black, even though his appearance remained white in color.

Many Latinos who immigrate to the United States consider themselves to be White, having been called White all of their lives. Upon arriving in the United States, many begin thinking of themselves as Brown or Black and call themselves Latino. What people in Brazil consider to be White, for example, is often not what people in the United States consider to be White. When people reach the United States, they sometimes have to adjust their racial thinking and racial identity to fit the new social environment. Different societies divide up the color continuum differently. All of this indicates that race is socially constructed—that is, created by people. If race were solely based in biology, something that we only objectively labeled by skin color, for example, Whiteness would be the same in all countries and there would be no need to negotiate a person's racial category. It would be obvious. People in different racial categories would be clearly distinct in terms of skin color. But because race is socially constructed with respect to how people perceive and understand biological features, it is highly flexible, changeable, and dynamic over time and in different locations, and millions of people have the same skin color but identify with different racial categories.

RACIAL FORMATIONS

Every country has a population with a certain degree of skin color variation. Over time, people decide how to categorize that range of skin color in their society and each society comes up with a slightly different racial categorization system. This process of determining the racial categories in to which people can place themselves is called **racial formations** (Omi and Winant 1994). Powerful social institutions and powerful groups determine the racial categories from which people can choose and identity their race. The U.S. Census has changed its set of racial categories more than 10 times. Some categories appear, disappear, and appear again, such as the category "Korean." It appeared in 1930, disappeared in 1950, and reappeared in 2000. Also in 2000, after years of deliberation, the Census decided to give people the option to mark all of the racial categories that they felt applied to them, allowing multiracial people to better identify themselves. This change also legitimated a multiracial status among the general population and the result was that more and more people began to identify themselves as biracial or multiracial instead of identifying with only one racial category, even though their genetic makeup and skin color did not change. The names of the racial categories have also changed over time, such as going from non-taxed Indian to Indian to American Indian, or from Negro to Black or African American. By implication, the way individuals identified their race also changed as these categories changed. This indicates that among the general public, as new racial categories emerge people change their racial identity, even though their biological features such as genetics and skin color remain the same. As an example, after the Black Power movement of the 1960s, more people referred to themselves as Black rather than Negro. After the Asian social movements of the 1970s, the term Asian-American became popular. Thus, through these processes of racial formation, race is constructed in the United States and people get to identify with one of the negotiated racial categories. They do not get to make up their own racial category.

CHECK POINT: Why is race a social construction—that is, made up by humans rather than just a process of labeling something objective?

Current U.S. Population Distribution by Race and Ethnicity

Before the 1960s Census, census-takers chose a race category for people (Cohn 2010). Since then Americans have been allowed to self-identify with respect to their race and even to choose more than one race. Below is the racial and ethnic distribution of the United States for 2010 from the U.S. Census.

Race/Ethnicity	Percent of the Total U.S. Population
White	72.4
Black or African American	12.6
American Indian and Alask Native	0.9
Asian	4.8
Native Hawaiian and Other Pacific Islander	0.2
Some Other Race	6.2
Two or More Races	2.9
Hispanic or Latino (Of Any Race)	16.3

There are several items to note in this table. The numbers represent people who self-identified, as opposed to being ascribed a race or ethnicity, like in the past. The White category includes Latinos. Non-Hispanic Whites account for 63 percent of the U.S. population. Latinos may be of any race because they are an ethnicity and currently the largest minority group in the United States. Other ethnicities would include Jews, Germans, the Irish, Arabs, and Norwegians, to name just a few.

Another aspect to note in the table is that multiracial individuals account for 2.9 percent of the U.S. population. By 2050, scholars estimate that they may reach as high as 20 percent because of immigration, interracial marriages, and growing acceptance of a multiracial status. Also, as a result of immigration and the birth rates among different racial groups, scholars predict that sometime between 2040 and 2050 the non-Hispanic White population will constitute slightly less than 50 percent of the population. Non-Hispanic Whites will remain the largest racial group—that is, no other single racial group will have as many people as them—and they will likely continue to hold most positions of authority in the country's important social institutions; but, when all of the minority groups are combined, the country will become a majority-minority nation, where the combination of minorities will add up to the majority of the populace, at over 50 percent.

The two groups with the largest immigrant populations are Latinos, especially from Mexico, and Asians, especially from China and Japan. Both groups are expected to see their populations more than double within the next 30 to 40 years due to immigration flows and birth rates. Although new immigrants often come from non-English-speaking countries, they have typically learned conversational English within 10 years of arriving in the United States. Their traditional destinations have been large coastal cities, such as San Diego, Los Angeles, Miami, and New York. However, more recently, immigrant populations have spread to nontraditional locations in the South and Midwest. One reason for this change in destinations is likely the expanding economies and manufacturing jobs. Although there are many unauthorized immigrants in the United States, the number fluctuates by the year and month, as a result of changing economic conditions. The number of unauthorized immigrants is estimated from a variety of sources, including the U.S. Census and the rate of captures by the Immigration and Naturalization Service. However, only a little over half of them enter through the borders, particularly from Mexico. Others usually come from overseas and enter the United States with legal papers, such as student visas or temporary work permits. Then they remain in the country after their papers expire. Consequently, many scholars and officials prefer to use the term *unauthorized immigrant* instead of illegal or undocumented immigrant because the immigrant may have entered legally and does have documentation. Or, an immigrant may have some forms of documentation, but not enough to be considered a legal immigrant at a certain point in time. The categorization of legal immigrant is complex in the current period.

It is very likely that the company for which you will work will have a racially and ethnically diverse workforce. If it does not, it will likely be open to having a more diverse workforce. Understanding that race is not biological but social will help in the sense of knowing that race and ethnicity are extremely personal forms of identity. They come with cultural and group associations. So, there is a balance between promoting a color-blind workplace and one that appreciates the history and emotion that support each racial and ethnic category. In fact, some scholars argue that favoring the idea of color-blindness actually results in more racism—color-blind racism—because it denies the structural aspects of racial inequality and ignores the personal importance of racial identity (Bonilla-Silva 2006). Learning about different racial and ethnic groups and their importance to coworkers, bosses, employees, and clients will make you a more valuable employee.

Racial and Ethnic Inequality

In addition to the racial categorization process that determines the available racial categories, it also attaches social characteristics to the categories. For example, the category of Asian tends to be associated with being the model minority, and with being intelligent. Asians are not associated with excellence in certain mainstream sports, such as football and basketball. In contrast, the category for Black or African American is often associated with a great ability in football and basketball, but not with intelligence or with the idea of a model minority. In large part, due to these associations, there is a significant amount of racial and ethnic inequality in the United States. **Racial and ethnic inequality** refers to the idea that some racial and ethnic categories are given certain types and amounts

© 2014 El Greco. Used under license of Shutterstock, Inc.

of resources while other categories are limited from them or denied them. As a result, there emerges a racial and ethnic hierarchy in the United States—that is, racial and ethnic statuses become important dimensions of social stratification. In most cases, U.S. non-Hispanic Whites are placed at the top of the ethnoracial hierarchy. Consequently, there is a gap in resources between non-Hispanic Whites and other racial and ethnic groups. The following charts exhibit these gaps.

	Median Net Worth in 2011 Dollars (Census Table 1 for Household Assets)
Total	68,828
Non-Hispanic White	110,500
Black	6,314
Asian	89,339
Other	19,023
Hispanic	7,683

	Median Family Income in 2009 Dollars (Census Table 697)
All Families	60,088
White	62,545
Black	38,409
Asian, Pacific Islander	75,027
Hispanic	39,730

	Percent of Persons Below the Poverty Level in 2009 (Census Table 715)
All Races	11.1
White	9.3
Black	22.7
Asian, Pacific Islander	9.4
Hispanic	22.7

	College Graduate or More in Percent, 2010 (Census Table 229)
All Races	29.9
White	30.3
Black	19.8
Asian, Pacific Islander	52.4
Hispanic	13.9

	Homeownership Rates First Quarter, 2012 (Census Table 7)
United States	65.4
Non-Hispanic White	73.5
Black	43.1
All Other Races	55.1
Hispanic	46.3

The Census tables show some notable outcomes. The median wealth of non-Hispanic Whites is considerably more than that of Asians and greater than 10 times that of Blacks and Hispanics. Whites also have a relatively high median income. However, Asians/ Pacific Islanders have an even higher median income, in large part because of the incomes of Chinese and Japanese Americans. Another reason is educational attainment. More than 50 percent of the Asian/Pacific Islander population has a college degree, which facilitates attaining a well-paying job. Whites and Asians/Pacific Islanders have the lowest percentages of people in poverty—more than twice as low as Blacks and Hispanics. Finally, the majority of non-Hispanic Whites own a home.

thinking *critically*

In what ways does homeownership increase a person's socioeconomic status?

Homeownership is particularly important for a few reasons. Much of middle-class wealth is in the value of the home, which typically appreciates in value over time. Homeowners are able to transfer wealth through their home. Residential areas filled with houses typically pay more property taxes that fund schools. Children who live in homes are therefore more likely to attend relatively well-funded schools, which help propel them on to college and well-paying jobs. Finally, the living arrangements inside the home (e.g., space and noise from neighbors) and activity outside the home typically offer comparatively low levels of stress, creating a psychological benefit as well.

Theoretical Explanations of the Socioeconomic Gap between Whites and Blacks

As the data from the Census show, there are gaps between Whites and minorities. That is, the groups are not equal in terms of many important socioeconomic characteristics. But the size of the gaps varies by the two groups being compared. It is important to note that the explanations for the gaps between Whites and a particular minority group will differ based on the minority group because each minority group has had a different historical experience in the United States. In terms of explaining the **Black-White gap**, there are four general explanations: culture of poverty, residential segregation, social structural change, and racism.

As already discussed, the idea behind the culture of poverty perspective is that the target group's culture causes them to be unsuccessful in society. In this case, the argument targets Black culture. According to this perspective, Black culture is different and has a negative effect on Blacks. There is some evidence suggesting that a percentage of Blacks take an oppositional stance toward society, such as not wanting to complete school or work at a typical 9 to 5 job (Anderson 1999). At the same time, that evidence also shows that the oppositional culture is a result of the deleterious structural surroundings, meaning that environmental factors are causing the culture as people respond to their social situation, rather than the culture building up a negative environment. The majority of Blacks do hold mainstream cultural ideals and a percentage of Whites do not. The cultural explanation for the gap between Whites and Blacks therefore leaves much to be desired. It may offer some insight into why some Blacks, as well as some Whites, remain in poverty, but is less explanatory with respect to explaining how they got into poverty and why there is a socioeconomic gap between Whites and Blacks.

Massey and Denton (1993) argued that an important explanation is residential segregation. Blacks are highly segregated from other racial groups in general, especially from Whites, and in some urban areas they are completely segregated from other racial groups. That is, they live in areas where 100 percent of the residents are Black. Residential segregation results in fewer job opportunities, less money to fund school districts, less police protection, fewer health care facilities, and less political power in the city. Other minority groups, such as Asians, which are comparatively integrated with Whites, are able to benefit from Whites' well-funded social institutions. Whites are much more willing to live in neighborhoods with Asians than with Blacks. In many places, White flight will occur when a single Black family moves into a neighborhood. There is some evidence suggesting that, for Whites, having 30 percent of their neighbors identify as Black is the threshold for moving to a new neighborhood. Then, when the national economy turns negative, Black segregated communities are hit harder than integrated neighborhoods, making recovery time even longer and more difficult for Blacks than other racial groups. The result is that, for many Blacks, it may take years or decades to recover from a recession and pass on wealth to future generations, explaining the socioeconomic gap between Whites and Blacks. Additionally, this residential segregation is typically not by choice. The majority of Blacks appear to be willing to live in, and even prefer to live in, integrated neighborhoods (Massey and Denton 1993).

William Julius Wilson (1996) also made a structural argument. During the 1970s and 1980s, the United States transformed from a manufacturing economy into a service economy, in large part due to new technologies, such as the personal computer. The United States began to import more of its goods, such as clothing and cars, leading to the disappearance of manufacturing jobs. These were the types of jobs that many Black men held and on which they were able to make a livable wage. With the disappearance of manufacturing jobs, work disappeared and so did accompanying income. Whites were not as affected by this transformation because they held a comparatively greater variety of jobs. Whites also had the financial and social resources to build new skills through attaining more education, which was not as viable an option for Blacks because of lack of overall wealth and the property tax system of funding quality schools.

Another explanation for the gap between Whites and Blacks is racism. There are a number of different definitions of racism. One definition is that **racism** consists of prejudicial attitudes and discriminatory actions toward a racial category or categories of people. **Prejudice** refers to negative opinions, beliefs, and emotions, while **discrimination** refers to negative behaviors at the individual and institutional levels. People may be prejudiced but not discriminatory. That is, they may hold a negative attitude toward a group of people but do very little in the way of showing it. People may also consciously discriminate against members of a group without being prejudiced toward them. There is evidence that some real estate agents hold no prejudices against Blacks, but at the same time they do not show Black clients all of the houses on the market because they do not want to disrupt relationships with other clients and potential clients. Then, there are people that are racist in the sense of being prejudiced toward a group and discriminate against them. Studies have found that Blacks are shown around half of the houses or rentals that are shown to Whites and receive about half as much credit assistance as Whites (Massey 2001). Other research finds that Blacks are half as likely to receive a call back for a job or a job offer compared to Whites when their resumes are exactly the same, with the only difference being a Black sounding name versus a White sounding name (Pager et al. 2009). Black applicants with no criminal histories actually receive fewer positive responses from employers than White applicants who report past felonies. Individual and institutional racism are unfortunately still occurring in the current time period, accounting for much of the socioeconomic gap between Whites and Blacks.

CHECK POINT: What is racism?

thinking *critically*

What would explain the differences between the socioeconomic status of Whites and other ethnoracial minorities, such as Latinos, Asians, and Native Americans?

SUMMARY

Although race seems to be objectively biological, it is based on society's socially constructed ideas about biology. Race is a social construction—something created by humans—and so racial categories change over time and are different in different societies. One way to know that race is ultimately social is to use the concepts of between-group variation and within-group variation. If racial categories were only a reflection of naming different inward or outward aspects of human biology, we would expect to see everyone in one racial category be objectively and clearly different from everyone in a second racial category. We would also expect to see very little variation among members of the same racial category. What we find in reality is the opposite—less variation between different groups in terms of skin color and more variation in skin color within a group. That is, there are millions of people who have the same skin color, such as light brown, but consider themselves to be White or Black or Asian or Latino or Native American. Being in separate racial categories should not happen if biological differences determine a person's racial identity. Since race is determined by societies through the processes of racial formations, race and ethnicity become dimensions of social stratification and result in racial and ethnic inequality. Whites typically enjoy the most resources in the United States, including wealth and homeownership. There are many explanations for the socioeconomic gap between Whites and ethnoracial minorities, but the particular factors vary depending on the specific racial or ethnic minority group of interest because each ethnoracial minority group has had different experiences, and currently has different experiences, in the United States.

Suggested Reading:

Pager, Devah, Bruce Western, and Bart Bonikowski. 2009. "Discrimination in a Low-Wage Labor Market: A Field Experiment." *American Sociological Review* 74:777-799.

ACTIVE LEARNING PROJECTS

In Class:

1. Pretend that tomorrow you woke up with a different race (pick one) and write about ways that your life would be different.
2. In a small group, list some movies and estimate how many characters were racial minorities. What were their characters like and what did they do? Discuss why.
3. Watch the video *Race: The Power of an Illusion* and in a small group discuss its main arguments and why the concepts of between-group variation and within-group variation matter with respect to race as a social construct.
4. In a small group, discuss how racial discrimination against minorities has negative effects on minority individuals, families, and communities, and discuss ways it has negative effects on White individuals, families, and communities.

5. Watch the video *True Colors: Racial Discrimination in Everyday Life*, with host Diane Sawyer, and in a small group discuss what occurs, why it occurs, and to what extent you think it happens today and in your area.

Out of Class:

1. Find a variety of magazines, or children's picture books, young adult or adult books, or movie posters, and count how many people are in them and then how many of the people are racial minorities. What is the percentage? Does it match the demographic percentage of that group in the United States, based on Census data? Write an essay about the differences, possible explanations, and whether it was easy or hard to visually categorize people into race and ethnic groups and why it was difficult or easy.
2. Pretend to write a letter to your newspaper's editor on the topic of racial inequality, giving examples, and explain why it is a problem for racial minorities and for Whites in particular. Offer potential solutions.
3. Go to a public food court or restaurant and listen and observe for any words or actions that may qualify as prejudice or discrimination. Write about the experience.
4. Research a local or national event involving racial conflict, inequality, or reconciliation and write an essay describing its main points, why it happened, and what can be learned from it.
5. In writing, brainstorm what it would be like, or what it was like if you did, bring a romantic partner home to your family for the holidays who was a different race than you. Explore why the interactions might go, or did go, that way.

KEY TERMS

Between-group variation	Prejudice	Racism
Black-White gap	Race	Within-group variation
Discrimination	Racial and ethnic inequality	
Ethnicity	Racial formations	

chapter 11

Gender Inequality

- Sex refers to the biological differences between men and women, while gender refers to the sociocultural symbols, characteristics, and behaviors that society ascribes to men and women.
- The idea that there are only two biological sex categories—male and female—is a social construction, as intersex individuals, who have a combination of male and female anatomy, exemplify because they do not fit neatly into either category.
- People develop a gender identity and learn their gender roles through participation in social institutions.
- Gender inequality is explained by a feminist perspective and a number of theories.

BE ABLE TO: Recognize gendered behaviors and gender inequality in your personal surroundings.

BIOLOGICAL SEX AND GENDER

When we walk in a populated area, we most likely assume that we know everyone's biological sex, taking it for granted that someone is either male or female. There are various clues that help us decide, such as facial characteristics, clothing, and movements. At times, we may also consider someone to be attractive. In the United States, the stereotypical attributes that mark a female as attractive include long hair, smooth facial skin, slim body, and long legs. The stereotypical attributes that mark a male as attractive include height, short hair, strong face, white teeth, muscular body, and appearing tough. Take a look at these pictures of two women and two men and decide to what extent they meet the stereotypical attributes of men and women in the United States and identify the clues that helped you come to that conclusion.

1.

© 2014 AlexAnnaButs. Used under license of Shutterstock, Inc.

2.

© 2014 CREATISTA. Used under license of Shutterstock, Inc.

3.

© 2014 photobank.ch. Used under license of Shutterstock, Inc.

4.

© 2014 Iancu Cristian. Used under license fo Shutterstock, Inc.

Which people did you assume were male and which people did you assume were female? If you chose pictures 1 and 3 as being male and pictures 2 and 4 as being female, you were correct. Sometimes it seems easy to spot a male or a female. But other times it is more difficult.

thinking *critically*

Why is it difficult sometimes, at least at first glance, to know whether someone is male or female?

We have learned to read certain cultural symbols that mark someone as being either male or female, but sometimes the other person mixes and matches the cultural symbols, making his or her appearance hard to read.

This gets to the difference between sex and gender. **Sex** refers to the biological differences between men and women. **Gender** refers to the sociocultural symbols, characteristics, and behaviors that society ascribes to men and women. Gender is a social construction. As a society, we decide what symbols, characteristics, and behaviors signify a male and a female. These things vary over time and are different in different locations. We interact with people based on their gender, and we only assume that we know their sex. Sex is typically thought of as fixed—that is, men and women should be biologically the same today as yesterday and here as well as there. Four of the main components of determining whether someone is male or female are (1) the chromosomes of XY for males and XX for females, (2) the hormone levels of estrogen for females and testosterone for males, (3) the organs of testes for males and ovaries for females, and (4) the differences in genitalia. The Census reports that in 2012 the percentage of women in the

United States was 50.8 and men, 49.2. Assuming there was no societal intervention, we would expect these numbers to be similar for other societies across time and space.

CHECK POINT: What is the difference between gender and sex?

Although it is important to keep the concept of biological sex separate from the concept of gender, even the idea of biological sex is influenced by society. To illustrate this point, intersexed individuals technically would not fit into either the male or female category. **Intersex** individuals have a combination of the standard biological differences between men and women. For example, some of them have XX chromosomes, typically thought of as female, with testes, or male genitalia with ovaries, or a variety of other combinations at the levels of genotype, internal organs, and outward physical features. Depending on the definition, the evidence suggests that 1 out of every 500 to 1,500 people are born with intersex characteristics, and these are probably conservative numbers (Dreger 1998). If we use the number of 1 out of every 500 people, there would be approximately 600,000 intersex individuals living in the United States today. To give that number a little context, it represents a similar number of people who live in the cities of St. Paul, Minnesota and Cincinnati, Ohio combined. It is a significant number. Based solely on the popular definition of biological sex, they would not fit into either the male or female sex categories. When filling out forms, should they write male or female? When going to the restroom, should they go to the men's room or women's room? Our society is only recently coming to acknowledge intersex individuals.

Other groups of people also call into question simple definitions of sex. **Transgenderism** is a state of gender identity where a person has the assigned biological features of one sex but feels like another sex. **Transsexualism** is the condition of changing sexual categories to align with psychological feelings through a transformation in appearance and activities, and in some cases through sex reassignment surgery. Transgenderism and transsexualism are separate from intersexuality because they do not have intersexed characteristics, at least at the levels of organs and genitalia. However, they also illustrate our society's current limitations in recognizing biological variation with respect to sex. Biologically, there are not only two fixed categories but rather a range of conditions and therefore a range of many potential categories.

thinking *critically*

Where in life do we learn that there are only two sexes?

THE SOCIAL CONSTRUCTION OF THE TWO-SEX CATEGORY SYSTEM

Having only two categories for sex is a social construction because, biologically, our society could have many more categories. The social institution of health care has policies on what to do if a baby is born with intersex features. A primary option is to conduct medical operations and initiate specialized drug use to make the person fit into one of the two socially constructed sex categories—that is, cause objective biology to match our subjective perceptions of biology, even before

© 2014 Ashley van Dyck. Used under license of Shutterstock, Inc.

the baby is able to decide for oneself. Many other social institutions have socialized us to believe that there are only two sex categories. The government's system of laws is set up for only two sex options, legitimating the **two-sex category system**. The mass media shows us only two sex categories and glamorizes the binary of sex through romantic comedies and news reports. Many religions tell us that the two-sex category system is sacred and spiritually ordained. The institution of the family typically passes on the traditional view that there are only two sex categories, through conservations, questions, jokes, and expectations. The institution of sports separates people into only two sex categories and often erupts into mean-spirited debate if that system is broken, because it is argued that someone may have an unfair advantage. As an example of this, Caster Semenya is a middle-distance runner who won the World Championships in 2009 and who took a silver medal in the 2012 summer Olympics. Competitors questioned her sex, and great controversy ensued, with the International Association of Athletics Federations conducting a deceptive and poorly handled investigation into the matter. They decided to let her race but have kept the findings sealed. Her response was that God made her the way that she is and she accepts it. Sara Gronert is a tennis pro on the women's circuit who was born with intersex features. Other tennis players complained that she was winning because of her male characteristics. Even though the World Tennis Association decided to let her remain in the women's league, she had surgery to discard the male characteristics and, in the minds of others, become a real or complete woman. As these examples suggest, there could be more than two categories to define biological sex. Yet, people in the United States are trained to think in a binary system regarding biological sex and the powerful institutions are structured for only two sex categories.

Gender Identity and Gender Roles

In the process of defining biological sex, large social institutions also create a picture of what a real woman and a real man look like and do. They shape ideas about femininity and masculinity. As individuals within these spheres, we develop **gender identities**, which are personal conceptions of what it means to be a male or a female. We also take on **gender roles**, which are society-ascribed and culturally expected behaviors for a man and a woman. These identities and roles change over time and by special context. For example, 100 years ago, U.S. society did not think that women were intellectually and emotionally capable enough to vote. Today, few people question a woman's ability to vote. The majority of U.S. citizens even assume that a woman will be president within their lifetime (Pew Research Center 2008). Such a possibility was not even considered until recently. In the 1950s, the pressure was for women to be homemakers.

There are also differences across space, such as differences by country. In the Philippines, it is normal for two heterosexual men to hold hands while talking. Two heterosexual men holding hands in the United States would typically generate confusion for people. In Scotland, men sometimes wear kilts. In the United States, many men may find a kilt to be too similar to a dress for comfort. These examples highlight that gender identities and roles are shaped by different societies in different time periods and that new generations of people are required to learn to be feminine or masculine.

CHECK POINT: What is the difference between gender identities and gender roles?

Gender and Biology

Although there is much social science evidence indicating that men and women act based on socialization processes, many people in the United States point to biology as the foundation of the differences between male and female behavior. Since humans are biological beings and people we typically identify as men and women have objective differences in DNA, hormone levels and physical features, some behavioral differences likely have origins in biology. Ultimately, gendered behavior is a combination of biology and society. Yet, if biology more than anything else determined gendered behavior, we would expect to see a large difference between men and women and only a small difference between all women and between all men with respect to a particular behavior. These differences between the sexes and similarities of members in each sex would also need to be fairly constant over time, since biology changes very slowly in this matter, and be similar in different countries, since we are all Homo sapiens.

The empirical evidence, however, shows much smaller variation between men and women than may be thought and great differences between members of the same sex group, especially when looking at societies across the globe. For example, in the United States in the 1800s, at least 10 percent of physicians were female, and there were many more practicing herbal medicine. Yet, by 1905, the percentage of female physicians declined to 4 percent and being a doctor became associated with masculinity. This lasted for over 60 years until the women's movement and then the percentage grew to 8 percent by 1970 and 24 percent by 2000 (Groves 2008). In 2011, 34 percent of physicians were women (Bureau of Labor Statistics 2012b). Women also currently constitute 48 percent of medical school graduates, suggesting that the percentage of female physicians will continue to rise. When we examine the percentage of female physicians in other countries we also find great variation. Of industrialized countries, Japan has 14 percent while Finland has 51 percent female physicians.

At the same time, while nursing in the United States has been traditionally associated with femininity, the percentage of male nurses is increasing, for example from 3 percent in 1970 to about 10 percent in 2011. Nursing is beginning to lose its association with being a female occupation. What these changes in percentages over time and across space illustrate is that women and men have the biological capability and desire to become physicians and nurses but that society more than biology plays the major role in determining the behavior to become a doctor or nurse.

CULTURAL TRANSMISSION THEORY AND COGNITIVE DEVELOPMENT THEORY

Two theories that explain gender identity and role differences from a social perspective are cultural transmission theory and cognitive development theory. **Cultural transmission theory** suggests that individuals are socialized from infancy to form a gender identity and take on gendered roles which the caretakers, such as parents, teachers, and coaches, believe are appropriate based on the gendered standards and expectations of the society. One experiment involved bringing a baby into a room to play with the study subjects (Gleitman et al. 2000). When participants were told that the baby was a boy, they offered him many toys and played with him vigorously. When they were told that the baby was a girl, they offered her a doll and touched her gently. Unbeknownst to them, it was the same baby both times. The differences in interaction depending on whether the baby was designated as a boy or a girl gave a glimpse into gender socialization processes that begin very early in life. Cultural transmission theory argues that the gender socialization process takes many years and constant reinforcement. It also assumes that individuals are passive receivers of these gendered lessons. **Cognitive development theory** argues that children are not only passive receivers but also seek out gender identities and roles. They come to identify as male or female in the first years of their life and attempt to learn the cultural characteristics and behaviors that are associated with each sex category. They begin to form their behavior and attitudes according to their perceived expectations of that particular gender, from pretending to be superheroes to playing house. Over time, people develop a gender identity and take on gendered roles.

GENDER INEQUALITY

Importantly, society does not only differentiate between men and women, giving them separate gender identities and roles, but also rewards them differently, typically recompensing male gender identities and roles over female, leading to **gender inequality**. While the Census reports that 27 percent of U.S. females have a bachelor degree or higher, compared to 28 percent for men, more men have doctorate or professional degrees. The Department of Labor reports that 47 percent of the labor force is female. Approximately 73 percent of employed women worked full time whereas approximately 90 percent of employed men worked full time. However, in 2009, the median earnings of men were $45,485 compared to $35,549 for women.

"You own this millenium."

Even when women work in the same occupation they are paid less than men. For example, the category of physicians and surgeons is the highest paid occupational category for women but they make about $12,000 less than male physicians and surgeons on average, even when working the same hours with the same qualifications. This difference results in an earnings gap of more than $360,000 over a career (Taylor 2012). Approximately 14 percent of women were in poverty in 2009, while 11 percent of men were in poverty. Lastly, the American Time Use survey documents that employed women spend about a half an hour more on housework each day than employed men and a larger percentage of women (83 percent) do housework each day compared to the percentage of men (65 percent).

thinking *critically*

Why is there an earnings gap between men and women?

Explaining the Earnings Gap between Men and Women

There are a number of explanations for the earnings gap between men and women. A primary one is a collection of theoretical ideas that fall under a **feminist perspective**, which argues for equality between men and women in society's social institutions. The fundamental arguments are that the United States continues to support a **patriarchal social system** that gives more power to men than to women in consequential social institutions, such as politics, law, and the family. To see the earnings gap shrink, men's positions of power and privileged roles would need to be more balanced with women's positions. The feminist framework focuses on changing power structures rather than on changing personal characteristics, such as by becoming more competitive or ambitious.

Another aspect of the feminist framework is the argument that gender is a unique form of social stratification. It is unlike class inequality or race inequality because men and women interact and have interconnected roles in every other social institution, which is not the case with respect to class differences and race differences. The poor and the wealthy, Whites and minorities, are not forced to interact everyday with one another and do not always have interconnected roles in many social institutions. Because of this unique gender situation, it is more difficult to understand and solve the earnings gap between men and women. No one explanation or solution works for every social institution.

Additionally, the feminist perspective, or framework, highlights the intersectionality of gender inequality. While women are already less privileged than men in a patriarchal society, they are at a double disadvantage in terms of class because of the earnings gap. There is an intersection of disadvantage between gender and class. Many women are also racial minorities, which amplifies the disadvantage even more. These forms of intersecting inequality represent a **matrix of domination** (Collins 2000), which represents the interconnected social structures that oppress certain people in a multiplicative way. For example, employers may be hesitant to hire someone from a poor neighborhood or a racial minority or a woman, but may overcome the hesitation and hire one of these candidates anyway. Yet, if the potential employee is a racial minority woman from a poor neighborhood, the likelihood of being hired drops considerably.

The feminist framework also builds off of an intersectionality perspective with the concept of **cumulative disadvantage**. Inequality and oppression do not have a one-time effect, but rather have a cumulative effect over time. The woman who does not get hired falls further down the economic latter, which magnifies the negative stereotypes of being a minority and a female, making it even harder to find employment and to build enough wealth to enact possible solutions, such as buying a car for transportation or developing another skill set through more education. To not have a car and less education further complicates the situation. In other words, the disadvantages build on one another over time. Men at least have one form of stratification that does not hinder them.

Another explanation of the earnings gap is **gender socialization**. Both men and women are socialized to believe that each gender has certain attributes that make a person better or worse at something. Only a few decades ago, for example, people did not think that women had the physical constitution to do sports. One of the 1967 Boston Marathon organizers attempted to pull Kathrine Switzer out of the race because women were not allowed to run marathons at that time. More recently people argued that young girls should not wrestle and especially not against young boys, arguing that girls were not as strong and that it went against social conventions commonly accepted about how boys and girls should interact. Currently young girls are allowed to wrestle and are doing fine. At home and in the workplace, women are often considered to be more patient, less aggressive, and more

"You said if I wore more makeup
I would be taken more seriously."

© 2014 Cartoonresource. Used under license of Shutterstock, Inc.

giving. But this may not be due to biology as much as it is due to gender socialization. The effect is that many women come to see their talents and tastes for a certain occupation based on their gender ideology. They then enter positions and fields that help other people, such as assistants or caregivers, and these positions and fields tend to pay less. Then, when it comes time for promotion, both men and women likely see the work of women differently than they see the same work done by men. For example, Condry and Condry (1976) ran an experiment where they gave a 9-month-old baby a Jack-in-the-Box toy and told a group of participants that the baby was a boy and told another group of participants that the baby was a girl. After the Jack-in-the-box scared the baby and the baby began to cry, the participants explained why the baby was crying. The participants who believed that the baby was a boy explained that he was angry and the participants who believed that the baby was a girl explained that she was afraid. Even though it was the same baby, doing the same thing—crying—people interpreted the actions differently based on their perceptions of the baby's gender. This experiment suggests that differences in perceptions about different behaviors, from crying to being assertive, likely occur in adulthood and in the workplace as well.

Sociologists also explain the gap income between men and women by studying the extent that certain occupations are sex segregated. For example, more men are dentists and more women are teachers. More men are auto mechanics. More women are bookkeepers. More men are managers. More women are restaurant servers. Female-dominated occupations are typically paid less. Even if it is the same occupation but different categories, the female-dominated one will be paid less. For example, the Census reports that quality control inspectors for cat food factories, wherein most inspectors are female, are paid 33 percent less than the quality control inspectors for dog food factories, wherein most of the inspectors are men. Or, the top five paid actresses in 2012 earned between $18 million and $34 million, while the top five paid actors in 2012 earned between $33 million and $75 million. Also, when an occupation goes from male dominated to female dominated, it sees a drop in pay, while the opposite occurs when an occupation becomes more male dominated. Furthermore, in female-dominated occupations, men are often pushed up to authority positions, or, as Christine Williams (1992) says, they ride a glass escalator rather than hit a glass ceiling, while women in male-dominated fields experience a glass ceiling or sticky feet and many times experience sexual harassment. **Sexual harassment** is a concept that represents the act of making people experience unwanted sexual attention or being made to feel that the workplace is a hostile environment because of their sex.

JOB SKILLS: Controlling Sexual Harassment

The Equal Employment Opportunity Commission reports that there were over 11,000 cases of sexual harassment in 2011, 84 percent of which were filed by women and 16 percent by men. This number is likely very conservative because many people do not report experiences of harassment. For example, an ABC News/Washington Post poll finds that 25 percent of women say that they have experienced sexual harassment at their place of employment (Langer 2011). They may have experienced unwanted sexual attention or experienced a hostile environment because of their sex. Sexual harassment can happen at the individual or organizational level. It is in the best interest of both male and female employees to know before they begin the job what sexual harassment is, how to avoid harassing behaviors, and what to do if experiencing harassment.

Sexism also explains the earnings gap. **Sexism** refers to the process of favoring one gender over another, typically male over female, while explaining the biased behavior with cultural scripts about the biological differences between the two sexes. In the past, women were not allowed to be firefighters because they were considered too weak. After policy changes, both men and women were required to pass physical tests with the result that many women were able to become firefighters and many men were not. More recently, we have seen a similar change in the military regarding combat. The assumption that women would not be able to handle combat is changing, since many women spent a lot of time in combat situations but were not being given the credit or the pay to match their sacrifices.

Finally, **neoclassical economic theory** argues that women seek jobs with high starting pay, which often have less career advancement possibilities, because they often plan on leaving the labor force to take care of family. Then, when they return to the labor force, they are comparatively less experienced and knowledgeable as the men who remained in the labor force. Therefore, they are paid less due to their comparatively smaller amount of experience and human capital.

CHECK POINT: What are some reasons for the earnings gap between men and women?

SUMMARY

Gender is a social construction while sex refers to the biological differences between men and women. Intersex individuals, who have a combination of the biological characteristics of men and women, show that a two-category sex system is a social construction. We learn our gender identities and the gender roles we are supposed to play through powerful social institutions, which cultural transmission theory and cognitive development theory explain. The male gender is given more resources in society than the female gender. A feminist perspective explains this disparity by focusing on the concepts of patriarchy, matrixes of domination, and cumulative disadvantage. Other theoretical perspectives highlight gender socialization, occupation segregation, sexism, and neoclassical economics.

Suggested Reading:

West, Candace, and Don H. Zimmerman. 1987. "Doing Gender." *Gender and Society* 1:125-151.

ACTIVE LEARNING PROJECTS

In Class:

1. Write about what your life would be like if you woke up in the morning as a different sex or gender.
2. Make a list of as many sports stars, politicians, and movie stars as you can think of and count the number of women. If a gender difference exists, attempt to explain it.
3. In a small group, list the times and places a man is allowed to cry and discuss why these times and places are allowed and not other times and places.
4. Bring in a couple of magazines targeted to men and targeted to women. In a small group, discuss what they communicate to men and women and why.
5. Bring in the lyrics of songs from different genres (e.g., country music, rap, pop) and, in a small group, discuss the gender roles portrayed and promoted.

Out of Class:

1. Write a fictional scene of a marriage proposal or view a proposal on Youtube.com and discuss the gender roles and why they are that way.
2. Find some jokes from other countries involving men and women and, in an essay, discuss what they say about men and women in the culture.
3. Watch the video *Playing Unfair: The Media Image of the Female Athlete* and describe its main arguments. Use the theoretical ideas of structural functionalism, conflict theory, and symbolic interactionism to explain the social outcomes presented in the video.
4. Research an occupation that you find interesting and, in an essay, describe its characteristics and average salary for men and women. Using a feminist framework explain the differences or similarities in salary between men and women.
5. Research the debate about whether transgenderism is a mental illness and offer your own perspective in an essay.

KEY TERMS

Cognitive development theory	Gender role	Sexism
Cultural transmission theory	Gender socialization	Sexual harassment
Cumulative disadvantage	Intersex	Transgender
Feminist perspective	Matrix of domination	Transsexual
Gender	Neoclassical economic theory	Two-sex category system
Gender identity	Patriarchal social system	
Gender inequality	Sex	

PART **V**

Why Do Societies Change?

chapter 12

Population and the Environment

DEMOGRAPHY

Within the last 200 years, the global population has increased dramatically, going from around 1 billion people in 1800 to approximately 7 billion in 2010 (U.S. Census 2011). The population continues to grow at a significant rate with 3 to 4 babies born every second, which translates into 300,000 every day, on average.

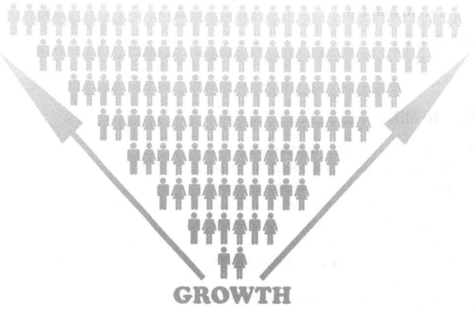

GROWTH

In 2010, the two most populated countries were China and India, each with over a billion people. The United States is the third most populated country with over 300 million people. In the United States, a baby is born every 8 seconds on average, which calculates to over 10,000 babies born every day. At the same time, there is also 1 death every 12 seconds, or a little over 7,000 deaths each day, on average. This would suggest that the United States is gaining over 3,000 new citizens every day. Yet, there is also a high rate of immigration and emigration, which represents foreign-born individuals coming into the country to live and also leaving the country. The level of migration changes from year to year, based on a variety of factors, including immigration policy and economic fluctuations. The field that studies these social dynamics is demography. **Demography** is the scientific study of the processes of fertility, mortality, and immigration in order to better understand the population components of size, composition, and density. Demography is a powerful tool in helping scholars and policymakers determine appropriate and beneficial social policies regarding a range of problems, including health care and disease, the global economy and poverty, and the environment. For example, demographers estimate that China has over 120 males to every 100 females.

thinking *critically*

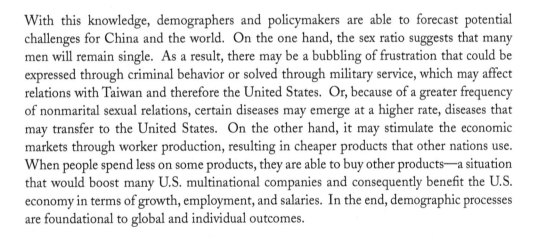

How could China's sex ratio influence you as an individual?

With this knowledge, demographers and policymakers are able to forecast potential challenges for China and the world. On the one hand, the sex ratio suggests that many men will remain single. As a result, there may be a bubbling of frustration that could be expressed through criminal behavior or solved through military service, which may affect relations with Taiwan and therefore the United States. Or, because of a greater frequency of nonmarital sexual relations, certain diseases may emerge at a higher rate, diseases that may transfer to the United States. On the other hand, it may stimulate the economic markets through worker production, resulting in cheaper products that other nations use. When people spend less on some products, they are able to buy other products—a situation that would boost many U.S. multinational companies and consequently benefit the U.S. economy in terms of growth, employment, and salaries. In the end, demographic processes are foundational to global and individual outcomes.

CHECK POINT: What is demography?

Fertility

In the field of demography, **fertility** refers to the behavior of having children. This is different from **fecundity**, which is the biological capacity to have children. Two of the most popular measures of fertility are the crude birth rate and the total fertility rate. The crude birth rate estimates the number of births per 1,000 people in the population. The total fertility rate is different than the crude birth rate because it does not consider the whole population but rather compares the number of births to age-specific groupings of women between the overall ages of 15 and 49. Very few babies are born to women outside these age boundaries and no babies are born to men, two aspects that make the crude birth rate less precise. With the total fertility rate, scholars arrive at a sense of the reproductive patterns in a society or the world. The world's total fertility rate has been on the decline for over 50 years and currently stands at 2.36 births per woman over her lifetime. The total U.S. fertility rate is 1.89. This number is below replacement, which suggests that the current generation is having fewer babies than what is needed to replace itself. In other words, even though U.S. women are still having a lot of babies, the U.S. population growth is slowing. Countries with some of the lowest TFRs include the Ukraine, the Czech Republic, and South Korea, while countries with some of the highest TFRs include the Democratic Republic of the Congo, Niger, and Angola.

Mortality

Depending on their country, individuals have a certain **longevity**, which is the average length of life of a person in a particular population, and a certain **life expectancy**, which is the average number of years left to live at any given age. When all countries are combined, the life expectancy at birth for individuals is 70 years—68 for men and 72 for women (Olson 2013). In the United States, a person can expect to live 78.62 years after birth—76 for men and 81 for women. Monaco has the highest life expectancy after birth at 89.63 years and Chad has the lowest at 49.07 years (Central Intelligence Agency 2013). Primary reasons for the stark differences between countries include diseases, famine, and health care systems. **Mortality** refers to the occurrence of death in a population, while **morbidity** represents the extent of sickness in a population. Scholars typically measure mortality with crude death rates, which calculate the number of deaths per 1,000 people in the population, and age-specific death rates, which account for the number of deaths per particular age groups. People in less developed countries often die from infectious diseases, such as HIV/AIDS, influenza, and pneumonia, as well as from sanitation problems and food shortages, while people in developed countries often die from chronic degenerative diseases. For example, in the United States, the number-one killer is heart disease and the most common form of heart disease is coronary artery disease, which can result in a heart attack. Approximately 750,000 people have a heart attack every year in the United States

(Centers for Disease Control 2013). A relatively close second cause of death in the United States is cancer. Heart disease and cancer account for over half of all deaths in the United States. There are differences between men and women for third place. For men, the third most common cause of death is accidents, particularly motor vehicle deaths and at younger ages. For women, it is cerebrovascular diseases, which affect the blood vessels that support the brain. Hypertension, for example, negatively affects the blood vessels and may lead to a stroke. Although genetics play a significant role in a person's overall health and well-being, a few behavioral and social solutions can extend longevity: eating healthily, exercising, and interacting with friends, all of which reduce stress.

MIGRATION

Migration affects the composition and density of the world's population but does not directly affect its size, only its distribution. However, migration does have a major impact on the population size of a country. **International migration** refers to the process of a person leaving one country to reside in another country. Some countries send a large number of migrants and some countries receive a large number of immigrants. The current estimates indicate that there are around 215 million international immigrants, or approximately 1 immigrant for every 33 people (International Organization for Migration 2013). The United States is typically the country that receives the most immigrants and Mexico sends the most migrants. Many of these immigrants voluntarily choose to travel to a new country, yet a little over 8 percent of them are forced out of their countries to become refugees—almost 50 percent of which are children. Usually, developing countries receive and send the most refugees, and currently Pakistan is hosting the largest number of them, adding up to over 1.5 million people, and Afghanistan is sending the most, over 2.5 million (United Nations Refugee Agency 2011). Other major sending countries include Iraq, Somalia, and Sudan, and other major receiving countries include Iran, Syria, and Germany. The United States hosts a little over 250,000 refugees.

thinking *critically*

Why do people immigrate to new countries?

Theories of Migration

There are a number of push and pull factors when it comes to international migration, referred to as **theories of migration**. Some forces push people out of their countries, from war to poor economies, and some forces pull people into receiving countries, from immigrant-friendly policies to employment opportunities. Neoclassical economic theory and new economics theory suggest that individuals and families run a rational cost-benefit analysis of sending one or two people from the family or the whole family to another country. They consider

"My startup could really use a pioneer type like you!"

the monetary, social, and physical costs of leaving against the possible rewards. When the calculus favors migration, many of them leave. These theories, however, are weaker in predicting where the immigrants will go.

Dual labor market theory argues that in industrialized countries there is a primary labor market, which contains jobs that pay well and are comfortable, and there is a secondary labor market, which contains jobs that are low paying and often physically demanding. Receiving countries that have large secondary labor markets are predicted to host a greater number of immigrants, who have the skills to obtain the secondary jobs but not the primary jobs.

World system theory examines the international global economic structure, pointing to wealthy countries drawing not only material resources from the poorer countries but also human resources. The flow of immigration therefore goes not only to specific countries that may have large secondary markets but to specific cities within the country, such as New York, Miami, and Los Angeles in the United States. As an example of the flow of human resources to specific places, sociologist Arlie Russell Hochschild (2001) describes a nanny chain. Los Angeles, for example, has many domestic servants, who come from a variety of places but especially from

Latin America. These domestic servants are almost all women and a significant portion of them have children of their own back in their country of origin. Consequently, the domestic servants take care of the children of the wealthy American families, giving them love that they would normally give to their own children. Their own children are being taken care of by other family members and babysitters, who also have children that in many cases are residing alone for the day. A chain of love is constructed where American children are receiving more love and other children in the chain are receiving less. As the world system theory argues, the power difference between countries has many unequal outcomes.

Finally, migration network theory explains that some countries, cities, and neighborhoods within the cities are chosen because the immigrants have social connections in those places, from primary or extended family to friends and acquaintances. These people offer social, cultural, and monetary support to help the immigrant adjust to and live in a new social environment.

EXPLAINING CHANGES IN POPULATION SIZE

Due to the processes of fertility, mortality and migration, each country's population is demographically different. Yet, what is the reason that populations grow or decline in size? One of the first scholars to systematically investigate this question was **Thomas Robert Malthus**, who lived in Great Britain from 1766 to 1834. He argued that populations can grow geometrically, as in 1 to 2, 2 to 4, 4 to 8, and 8 to 16. Or, in other words, if one woman has one child, there would be two people. If each of them had one child, there would be four people, and if those four people each had one child, then there would be eight people, and so on. At the same time, however, he argued that the food supply can only increase at an arithmetic rate, as in 1 to 2, 2 to 3, 3 to 4, and so forth. The real-world idea is that if there is one plot of land, only so much can be gleaned from it with respect to food. Production technology may get better but not to the point of having a geometric rate of subsistence. According to this theory, then, populations will increase in size until the geometric rate crosses over the arithmetic rate. Then, there will be food shortages and population decline. Malthus also posited preventive checks and positive checks to population growth. Preventive checks included behaviors, such as not having sexual relations before marriage and delaying marriage to older ages, or what he called vices, such as using birth control or engaging in homosexual activity. Positive checks included wars, famine, and epidemic diseases. Preventive checks were before population increases and positive checks were after population increases. Both types of checks would control each nation's population growth.

Although Malthusian ideas are still discussed today, most social scientists typically look to the demographic transition theory for an answer to why different countries and the world experience changes in population size. **Demographic transition theory** explains the change in population size by focusing on four stages of national transformation. In the first stage, a country has low technology and a preindustrial economy and consequently high fertility and mortality rates. The country also institutionalizes and supports practices that result in high fertility, to work the farm, for example. Then, the society begins to change through modernization, which decreases the mortality rate. Lower infant mortality rates and longer life expectancies result. However, the population still has a high fertility rate because of the social practices and values. The population grows in size. In the third stage, women begin to have greater power in society, gain higher rates of education, work in the labor force, take political offices, and choose to decrease the number of children they have, decreasing fertility rates. The population decreases in size. In the final stage, fertility and mortality rates are low, possibly to the point of experiencing negative growth. Many countries are currently experiencing this type of population decline, such as Japan and a number of European countries. With this theory, demographers are able to predict that the world population will begin to slow around 2050 and predictably decline after that because more and more developing countries will go through modernization stages and slow their population growth.

CHECK POINT: What are the four components of the demographic transition theory?

Job Skills: Searching for a Job

The life course perspective from Chapter 7 incorporates the idea of historical time in individual outcomes. Demography gives us a sense of our place in time and what we might expect in the future with respect to finding a job. For example, those born in 1950 were part of the baby boom generation. When they came of age, they had a lot of competition in finding a job. But if persons were born during the 2007–2009 recession or shortly thereafter, they will likely have comparatively less competition because birth rates decline during recessions. Consequently, finding a job may be more or less easy depending on the historical time, independent of each person's own ambition and intellectual prowess. Although such knowledge may not help directly in finding a job, it does offer some consolation in the level of difficulty in succeeding. Some things are out of the control of the individual and knowing these things may relieve some personal stress.

Population Policy

Population policies are government-instituted programs that attempt to directly or indirectly change population numbers. Governments may want to decrease, increase, or maintain their populations by focusing on fertility, mortality, or immigration. They may try a direct approach by creating specific programs, such as family planning programs, or they may create policies that reward or sanction citizens for having babies or for migrating. They may also take an indirect approach by modernizing certain parts of their economy, from manufacturing to education, which would affect fertility, mortality, and immigration rates. Or, they may change policies, such as equal employment laws, to allow women more power to lead influential programs, since women that have more institutional power have better control over their fertility. Governments may also run media campaigns to spread information about particular population problems. Even though the world population is growing, the populations of some countries, like Japan, are not. This situation makes it difficult for these countries to generate tax revenue and fill service and manufacturing jobs, from health care workers to construction workers. Consequently, different countries institute different population policies.

The Global Village and Global Inequality

Some scholars and activists have used the metaphor of a global village to give us a sense of the **global inequalities** between countries (see Kastle 2013 for an example). The concept is to shrink the world down to 100 people. In this village, 61 people would be from Asia, 15 from Africa, 10 from Europe, 9 from South America, and 5 from North America. The majority of them (82) would come from less developed countries and have an average income of around $5,500, equaling $15 a day. The other 18 villagers would come from developed countries and have an average income of around

$32,500, equaling $90 a day. Half of the village, however, would live on less than $2 a day. Additionally, 25 of the 100 villagers would live in poor housing or be homeless.

In the current state of global inequality, approximately 16 percent of the world was officially living in poverty in 2010, with 47 percent of Sub-Saharan Africa living in poverty while only 1.8 percent of Europe and Central Asia were living in poverty (Chandy and Gertz 2011). Yet, by other definitions, the United Nations Children's Fund (UNICEF) reports that out of the 2.2 billion children in the world, 1 billion are currently living in poverty and 22,000 die from hunger each day. The wealthiest 20 percent of people in the world own approximately 75 percent of the wealth while the poorest 40 percent own only 5 percent of the wealth (Shah 2013).

thinking *critically*

What are some ways that an individual could help to decrease global inequality?

THE ENVIRONMENT

In addition to populations having consequences for global inequality, they also put pressure on the natural environment. The **natural environment** refers to all the physical attributes of the earth below, on top of, and above the ground, consisting of living organisms and natural materials. Such things would include dirt, trees, animals, and air. People have always had a significant relationship with the natural environment, but it has not been until recently that they have had the power to drastically transform it to the point of making it uninhabitable. In many large cities, the air pollution is thick enough to be visible. The world's rainforests are being clear-cut at an astonishing rate. The size of landfills is expanding precipitously. Because there is only one natural environment, it is important to understand the extent to which humans change it and the extent to which it changes humans. **Ecology** is the study of organisms interacting with the environment. One measure of estimating the impact humans have on the environment is called the **ecological footprint**. It compares the human consumption of the environment with the capacity of the environment to replenish itself. That is, it estimates the amount of space a human would need to live to account for his or her consumption patterns. Typically, it is reported in hectares. One hectare is a little under 2 football fields in size. The Global Footprint Network (2013), which uses scientific methods to estimate the ecological footprint of countries and the world, reports that the average ecological footprint per person in the world is currently just over 2.5 hectares—that is, almost 4.75 football fields. This number suggests that the earth would need 1.5 years to regenerate the materials we use in a single year. We are therefore running a deficit to be sustainable. For the United States, the average ecological footprint per person is almost 7 hectares or a little over 13 football fields. In other words, Americans use approximately 180 percent more environmental materials than the global average and much more than can be sustainable in the long term.

Climate Change

One highly discussed environmental topic is **climate change**. The United States Environmental Protection Agency (2014) reports that the planet is warming, resulting in melting glaciers, rising sea levels, and acidic oceans, and that a significant contribution to this change is human activity. Through industry production and individual consumption, humans are generating large amounts of carbon dioxide that goes into the atmosphere. The result is a greenhouse effect where the sunlight comes in and the heat is trapped, creating a warmer environment. Even a 1-degree change in temperature creates warmer waters that affect sea life and overall weather patterns, from wildfires to hurricanes, which affect water supplies and agriculture, from crop output to farming that uses more pesticides. The ripple effects continue down to power and transportation systems, which affect international trade and monetary exchange. The national budgets and world economies are impacted, and consequently each individual experiences the effect of climate change. Among scientists, the debate no longer seems to be whether the planet is warming but rather what should be done about it. There has been some international unity with the Kyoto Protocol to reduce gas emissions and international conferences that include governments, environmental organizations, and individual scientists and activists. Yet, there remains a need for much greater action.

thinking *critically*

What have you heard about climate change and what do you believe and why?

The Impact on Humans

The negative effects of human activity on the environment in turn create an environment that is harmful to humans. The National Institute of Environmental Health Sciences and the Environmental Health Perspectives agency (2010) report that there are a number of health maladies resulting from the ripple effects of climate change, such as respiratory problems, cancer, neurological disorders, and water- and foodborne illnesses. For example, they find that with each centigrade degree increase in temperature, there is a 2.5 to 6 percent increase in the risk of foodborne illnesses, and that foodborne illnesses affect between 6 and 81 million people in the United States each year. Additionally, they report that thousands of deaths occur from hurricanes and typhoons and these weather events force hundreds of thousands of people to relocate, costing communities and governments billions of dollars. These outcomes also have powerful psychological effects, causing mental and emotional stress as well as interpersonal and family conflict that may last a lifetime. Moreover, the World Health Organization estimates that over 3 million people die prematurely, almost half of which are children under the age of 5, due to indoor and outdoor air pollution. Workplaces around the world expose approximately 125 million people to asbestos and a little over 100,000 people die from asbestos-related cancer each year. It is not surprising, therefore, that ecologists constantly remind people that humanity and the natural environment are extremely interconnected.

Environmental Justice

The negative effects of a polluted environment are not distributed equally across populations. **Environmental justice** refers to the equal treatment and involvement of all people regardless of social status with respect to realizing the protection of environmental laws and experiencing a safe natural environment. It also reflects a social movement that reveals the reality that minorities, particularly racial minorities and the poor, are exposed to more environmental hazards than other groups of people and, in accordance, it attempts to help them. The majority group holds the attitude of "not in my backyard" when it comes to the placement of hazardous waste, and they have the political and financial power to follow through on that attitude by ordering the hazardous waste to be

placed in areas far away from them. For example, Shriver and Webb (2009) document a carbon-black problem in a small Native American town in Oklahoma. Carbon-black is a rubber compound that leaves a residue of black powder when produced. In addition to the monetary costs of keeping their cars and homes clean from this black powder, Native Americans in the town have a high rate of respiratory problems. They also limit how often they visit friends and family outside of town and how often friends and family visit them in town to control the spread of the black powder. There are negative effects on the health of the community members as well as on the social strength of the community itself. The industry and political representatives, however, do very little to remedy the situation, and very little of the money made through the industry returns to the community. Due to the community members' economic standing they are often unable to relocate to a different town, or they want to stay because they feel attached to the town in which they have lived for years before the industry built the factory there. This situation may be called **environmental racism** or **environmental discrimination**, which represents the attitudes and behaviors of the majority group with respect to placing the burden of environmental waste mainly on minority groups.

Environmental Sustainability

Considering that the population of the world will grow for many more decades, requiring greater use of the natural environment, scholars and activists are organizing to create ways to solve environmental problems and live an **environmentally sustainable** existence. This means that people and industries will use only the amount—or less—of the environmental materials they need in a manner that would allow the earth to support human life indefinitely. In particular, Americans will need to develop a sustainable culture to reduce their consumption patterns and reorganize their industry regulations to decrease their ecological footprint. For example, currently the U.S. population makes up 4 percent of the world population, yet it consumes 19 percent of the world's primary energy (United States Energy Information Administration 2013). At the same time, because the United States is a high-income

nation and a major world power, it has the infrastructural, financial, and political means to solve many of the environmental problems and to encourage other countries to also live an environmentally sustainable lifestyle. Scholars note that the environmental problems and solutions are large enough to require an international coalition.

SUMMARY

Demography is the study of populations, particularly size, composition, and density, through the social processes of fertility, mortality, and migration. Fertility refers to the behavior of having children and mortality refers to the occurrence of dying. Globally, when there are more births than deaths, the global population increases. However, when examining specific countries, immigration is also important. People migrate to different countries for a variety of reasons, including the ideas that they will be better off economically and socially, that the receiving country has a large secondary labor market, that the global economic market puts pressure on individuals to migrate, and that immigrants have a social network that makes migrating easier. These demographic processes influence population change. Malthus argued that populations grow and decline in size because groups can increase geometrically while food supplies can increase only arithmetically. Populations grow until the food supply is not enough and then they shrink back down. But the demographic transition theory is currently the most empirically supported theory on population change. It argues that societies go through four stages of change as they modernize, growing and then declining in population. It has helped scholars be able to predict the world's population and when it will likely slow in growth and eventually decline. Individual countries also make population policies to either encourage or discourage population growth. In the end, there is global inequality among nations, where the majority of people share a minority of wealth.

Population dynamics are also consequential for the natural environment. As the world grows in size, the combination of nations may have an overall larger ecological footprint, which is a measure of consumption compared to the earth's ability to regenerate the desirable materials. At this point, the ecological footprint is not sustainable because in a year we use the amount of material that would take the earth a year and a half to replenish. Moreover, individual and industrial waste is causing long-term environmental damage. Through climate change studies, scientists have documented a temperature increase and noted some of the current and future consequences. These problems, however, do not only hurt the earth but because humans and the earth are so interconnected, the environment begins to harm people as well, particularly racial and class minorities. Environmental justice groups attempt to rectify this inequitable situation and to promote an environmentally sustainable lifestyle.

Suggested Reading:

Masters, Ryan K., Robert A. Hummer, and Daniel A. Powers. 2012. "Educational Differences in U.S. Adult Mortality: A Cohort Perspective." *American Sociological Review* 77:548-572.

ACTIVE LEARNING PROJECTS

In Class:

1. Look through magazines that target men and those that target women and summarize information regarding fertility issues, from pregnancies to contraception. Write answers to the following questions: Are they presenting different stories? Why or why not?
2. Think in your life about moving from one location to another or changing schools. Write answers to the following questions: What made you anxious or excited?

What might new immigrants to the United States be feeling and expecting?

3. In a small group, write down ideas about ways to make a college campus or a work office more environmentally friendly.

4. In a small group, decide on an environmental topic and create a poster that gives information on it.

5. Look on Google Images of political cartoons about the environment and create one of your own about an environmental issue.

Out of Class:

1. Pick a country and study its demographic characteristics and issues and create a presentation with the information.

2. Find out how much it costs in your community to get a casket or do a cremation, have a funeral, put an obituary in the newspaper, and any other item related to mortality.

3. Spend an hour picking up trash at a park or some other location and describe your feelings and thoughts about the experience before, during, and afterward.

4. Research an environmental issue in your area and write an essay describing it.

5. Create a weekly food plan that would be more environmentally sustainable than what you eat currently.

KEY TERMS

Climate change	Environmental sustainability	Morbidity
Demographic transition theory	Fecundity	Mortality
Demography	Fertility	Natural environment
Ecological footprint	Global inequality	Population policies
Ecology	International migration	Theories of migration
Environmental justice	Life expectancy	
Environmental racism/	Longevity	
discrimination	Malthus, Thomas Robert	

chapter 13

Deviance and Social Control

DEVIANCE

One of the most provocative celebrities is Lady Gaga. From her semiclothed videos to her eccentric costumes, she seems to consistently generate confusion, admiration, and controversy. In 2010, she wore a dress made completely of meat to the MTV Music Video Awards. She wanted to lift the ban on gays and lesbians serving openly in the U.S. military, arguing that people need to stand up for their rights or they will only be pieces of meat. Her behavior may be classified as deviant, even if her underlying motivation could be considered morally defensible. **Deviance** is any action that violates the behavioral expectations of a group or society. In other words, deviance reflects norm-breaking. Because groups and societies attach different degrees of importance to norms, they also attach different degrees of importance to deviant behavior. The degree of importance may depend on the type of action and how

© 2014 Helga Esteb. Used under license of Shutterstock, Inc.

far it deviates from the norm. In some cases, such as with a child interrupting an adult conversation, the behavior is likely to be only lightly reprimanded, while in other cases, such as detonating bombs in public places, the behavior may result in capital punishment. The group or society may decide that the consequence for the deviant behavior should be the person's death. Interrupting conversations and acts of terrorism are both examples of **negative deviance**, which is behavior that violates a norm. Yet, not all deviance challenges norms. In some cases, the deviant behavior attempts to meet social expectations. **Positive deviance** is over-conforming to the norm (Eitzen 1999). For example, a little league baseball pitcher who wants to meet the expectations of winning may practice throwing the ball so often that he or she gets injured. This pitcher engaged in positive deviance by over-conforming to the norm. The American cyclist Lance Armstrong used banned substances to win races, arguing that it was impossible to win the Tour de France without using drugs during his time, because all of the top riders were doping (Leicester 2013). Arguably, he exemplifies both negative and positive deviance, because doping is typically considered a reflection of negative deviance but using them to win may be a sign of going beyond the norm of doing well to win—reflecting positive deviance. Other examples of positive deviance may be more benign. A father spends the majority of his time at work so that he can meet the provider expectation. A student may consistently study late into the night in order to meet grade expectations. They seem like positive actions, yet when they are taken too far away from the expected behavior they represent deviant behavior.

CHECK POINT: What is deviance?

Deviance Over Time and Space

Since deviance reflects norm-breaking, an action may be considered deviant in one time-period and not in another time-period. Or, the same action may be considered deviant to one group or society but not to another group or society. That is, there is no behavior that has always been considered deviant by all groups in all time periods. Fifty years ago, interracial couples were believed to be deviant, even by law in some states. Yet, the majority of Americans today accept such relationships. For some groups, engaging in sexual relations before marriage is deviant behavior, while other groups encourage it. Sociologists argue that no behavior is inherently immoral. Even the behaviors that Americans typically consider to be obviously wrong are actually only deviant relative to the context and group or society at the time. That is, in the right context at the right time, groups and societies do not consider the behavior to be immoral, wrong, or deviant. For instance, past societies have killed individuals to appease the gods. The United States killed 43 prisoners on death row in 2011. Royal families have committed incest to keep the bloodlines pure. Numerous people in the country of Mauritania currently own slaves and many people in the country, including many slaves, assume slave owners take sexual advantage of their slaves—in other words, actions one group would label rape, another group does not (Sutter 2012). Many countries use torture as a military tactic. Even in the United States, there was much debate about whether waterboarding was considered torture. Different groups saw the same action differently. Ancient Greeks valued homosexual relations between adult males and young boys, as does the current Papua New Guinea tribe, Etoro. Some groups find it tolerable and even morally righteous to burn the Bible or Koran or some other religious text. Using weapons of mass destruction, from nuclear bombs to improvised devices, are also considered necessary at certain times against certain people. Stealing, cheating, property destruction, domestic violence, corporal punishment, prostitution, human trafficking, drug use, and a list of other behaviors have all been, and are, acceptable to some groups at some times in history. That is, they are not considered deviant, depending on the situation. Individuals use cultural standards to evaluate their own and other people's behavior, making the morality and appropriateness of the behavior subjective rather than objective.

thinking *critically*

Can Santa Claus have one set of standards to judge whether everyone is naughty or nice?

ALCOHOL USE AMONG COLLEGE STUDENTS

Alcohol use among U.S. college students is prevalent. The National Institute of Alcohol Abuse and Alcoholism (2014) finds that 80 percent of college students drink alcohol and about 50 percent binge drink, which the Centers for Disease Control and Prevention define as five or more drinks for men and four or more drinks for women in 2 hours. Due to these numbers it would appear that college students do not consider alcohol use or binge drinking to be a deviant behavior, even though many administrators and people outside of the college environment often label it to be deviant behavior, especially for underage drinkers. Even though there may be subjective disagreement about what constitutes deviant behavior, the consequences of the behavior are objective—that is, they can be empirically collected. The NIAAA reports that 1,825 college students between the ages of 18 and 24 die from alcohol-related injuries every year. More than 690,000 college students are assaulted each year by someone who has been drinking and almost 100,000 students are victims of alcohol-related sexual assault. Over a quarter of students also miss class and do poorly on assignments or exams because of alcohol use.

SOCIAL CONTROL

For society to progress economically, socially, and politically, there needs to be a certain amount of social order. People must be able to coordinate their behaviors and to cooperate with each other. **Social control** refers to the task of preventing deviant behavior. All groups have a degree of social control because norms, by definition, have sanctions attached to them. When the norms are broken, that is, when deviance occurs, there are consequences. People in all social institutions, from the family to the government, react. **Informal social control** represents the casual techniques that get people to conform. These techniques may include a look or a change in voice, or something more consequential, such as violence or banishment. **Formal social control** represents the control strategies that have been institutionalized and are performed by persons in authority. For example, school administrators or police officers may suspend someone or give them a ticket. The formal social control is more consequential because it does not matter who plays the role of authority, the behavior has been identified and the consequences set. In many cases, an employer must dismiss someone for a certain action or a judge is forced to give a particular sentence for a specific crime, even when the specific employer or judge would rather not enact the required consequences.

| **CHECK POINT:** | What does social control mean? |

Laws and Crimes

Laws are formalized norms intended to control deviant behavior and **crimes** are violations of the formalized norms with generally agreed upon penalties. Given the range of deviant behavior, there is also a range of crime. Some scholars use the term **victimless crime** to denote the illegal actions of an individual that does not directly affect someone else or an illegal exchange between two willing parties. There are many people who argue that society should decriminalize some victimless crimes, such as marijuana use, prostitution, gambling, public nudity, driving without a helmet or seatbelt, underage drinking, and assisted suicide. They claim that such behavior will continue despite formal social controls and will only slow down the criminal justice system. Other people, however, argue that there are no victimless crimes. In an interconnected society, every action by one person affects someone else. For example, a person who smokes marijuana at home had to purchase it from someone, who had to get it from a trafficker, who had to get it from a producer. Additionally, the effects may require coworkers or family members to take over, or help with, jobs that they would not otherwise have to do. Some victimless crimes, such as public nudity or pornography, influence people's perceptions and reinforce stereotypes.

There are also crimes that society considers to be important enough to make the rate of incidences known to the public. The Federal Bureau of Investigation reports on eight

index crimes in their Uniform Crime Reports: the violent crimes of murder, rape, robbery, and assault; and the property crimes of burglary, theft, motor vehicle theft, and arson. Through these reports society has a sense of the trends in crime—whether the crime rate is going up or down. In the last two decades, the rates of crime have been declining, as reported by the FBI. The reports also offer information on the relationship between the perpetrator and the victim. The majority of victims know the offender.

Hate crimes, or bias-motivated crimes, are comparatively new in the sense of having their own label. Hate crimes are criminal actions against someone or someone's property based on bias against the person's race, religion, disability, ethnic/national origin, or sexual orientation. However, different U.S. states have laws for different forms of bias. The first state statutes for hate crimes were adopted in 1981in Washington and Oregon, but currently not all states have passed specific hate crime statutes (Shively 2005). Therefore, the protection against hate crimes varies widely by state. For example, 30 states have laws against crimes based on sexual orientation but only 10 states have laws against crimes based on transgender identity (Human Rights First 2013). Hate crime also likely goes underreported by victims and authorities because victims often lack the knowledge that an incident could be labeled a hate crime and many law enforcement personnel do not comply with the collection process for hate crimes. The hate crime rates consequently remain incomplete (Shively 2005).

White-collar crime is usually committed by business professionals or government workers who engage in some type of fraud or run a relatively complicated scam. Some examples are insurance and hedge fund fraud and timeshare and work-at-home scams. Two of the well-known cases are the energy company Enron that doctored its accounting books to make it look like it earned more money than it actually did and Bernard "Bernie" Madoff who constructed an investment Ponzi scheme where investors were paid with their own money or with money from new investors instead of from investment profits. Rather than white-collar crime directly affecting a single individual, as is the case with many street crimes, it has a wide-ranging impact because it can hurt thousands of families by costing them their jobs and life savings. For the fiscal year 2010–2011, the Federal Bureau of Investigation (2011) reported that they secured billions in restitution for each of the following white-collar crimes: financial institution fraud ($1.38 billion); mortgage fraud ($1.8 billion); corporate fraud ($2.4 billion), securities and commodities fraud ($8.8 billion), and health care fraud ($12 billion). They also secured millions in restitution for asset forfeiture/money laundering ($18.4 million) and insurance fraud ($87.6 million). These constitute only a few categories in one year's time, suggesting that there is likely more white-collar crime occurring than is prosecuted.

Comparatively few white-collar criminals are prosecuted, relative to street criminals, and sentences for white-collar crime tend to be comparatively light. Jeffery Skilling, the former chief executive officer of Enron, is currently serving a 14-year jail sentence for his participation in the accounting scandal. The fraud cost investors over $40 billion, of which they may have received around $10 billion in compensation after settlements, and 20,000 workers lost $2 billion in pensions, of which they were able to get back $85 million or about $3,500 for each employee after settlement fees (Axtman 2005). By comparison, most U.S. states have three-strikes laws. If a person has two prior felonies, or a misdemeanor that could be recategorized as a felony with a third conviction, he or she receives a mandatory minimum sentence of 25 years in jail. These felonies could include petty theft or drug possession. The result is that there are numerous people sentenced to longer jail terms than Jeffery Skilling for crimes that have a comparatively small effect on other individuals and society as a whole. Two explanations for the difference in sentencing is that white-collar crime is often highly complicated in terms of what was actually done and which aspects were illegal, and white-collar criminals are often wealthy, allowing them to hire highly experienced, well-funded, and skilled lawyers.

Prison Population

For the last 10 years, the U.S. prison population at state and federal levels has remained around 1.5 million people (Carson and Sabol 2012), which is about 0.5 percent of the total U.S. population. As of 2011, half of the prisoners at the state level were incarcerated for violent crimes and half of the prisoners at the federal level were incarcerated for drug offenses. The vast majority of inmates are under state jurisdiction (87 percent), and the vast majority are male (93 percent). With respect to male inmates, 36 percent are Black, 30 percent are White, and 22 percent are Hispanic. Most female inmates are White (49 percent). Most men and women are in jail for violent crimes, yet the percentage is much higher for men than women. Almost equal numbers of women are in jail for property crimes. In relative terms, more Whites are in jail for property crimes than drug-related crimes while more Blacks are in jail for drug-related crimes than property crimes. Hispanics are fairly split between property and drug-related crimes. Most inmates are also between the ages of 20 and 29 (29 percent) or 30 and 39 (30 percent). Overall, these statistics suggest that the U.S. prison population is mainly male ethnoracial minorities between 20 and 39 years old who committed a violent crime. One reason for this profile is that a high percentage of young racial and ethnic minorities live in structurally disadvantaged neighborhoods where schools are poorly funded, job opportunities are scarce, poverty is high, and access to health care is limited. Whites who live in similar environments have similar incarceration rates for violent crime (Peterson and Krivo 2005).

thinking *critically*

Why do people commit deviant acts and crime?

EXPLAINING DEVIANCE AND CRIME

For centuries, scholars have theorized about why people commit deviant behavior or commit crime. Some early explanations came from religious ideology, such as having a bad spirit or being possessed by a demon. Other early explanations focused on biological features, such as head shape and body hair, which were thought of as outward manifestations of inward deficiencies. Most scholars now examine social environmental impacts as potential causes of rule-breaking. Given that deviance and crime are based on cultural norms, Emile Durkheim argued that some people experience **anomie**. When they are unaware of, or unclear about, the cultural norms, or the cultural norms have weak sanctions, or they must choose between competing expectations, they are more likely to be considered a deviant or a criminal. These situations occur in areas that see a fast inflow of a diverse set of people, or in areas that experience a separation from the typical means of following the cultural norms. For example, stealing is breaking a cultural norm, but it is comparatively common in economically depressed areas. Robert Merton built on Durkheim's ideas with his **structural strain theory**. In brief, he argued that people in the United States are socialized to achieve wealth, yet not everyone is given the institutional means to realize that goal. Young adults are told to get an education, yet some schools are severally underfunded, underequipped, and understaffed. Students are then told to go to college and get a well-paying job, while they have received poor training, have no money for college, and live in an area with very few well-paying job opportunities. People in these situations respond in different ways. One response is to maintain the cultural goal and use non-institutionally accepted means, such as prostitution, drug dealing, and embezzlement, to achieve it. Another response is to reject both the cultural norms and the institutional means without replacing either of them with anything new, a response that Merton called *retreatism*. These individuals may become alcoholics or drug addicts or drop out of society in some other way. There are also the rebels. They reject the cultural norms and institutional means and devise new norms and means. They may start radical social movements, for example.

Edwin Sutherland's **differential association theory** focuses less on structural dynamics and more on interpersonal dynamics. Sutherland argued that people learn to be deviant by interacting with people who are acting in deviant ways. They not only learn how to act, such as how to smoke marijuana or to drink alcohol, but they also learn to hold attitudes that support such action. At the same time, associations with norm-conforming individuals keep people from acting in a deviant manner. Travis Hirschi's **control theory** extends this idea. He argues that people's attachments to certain individuals, from gang members to coaches, will be more effective with respect to changing someone's behavior when there is an emotional connection. People are also less likely to commit deviant acts when they are connected to society through organized groups, such as sports teams or clubs, because deviant acts could result in a loss of membership. Finally, the more commitment people make to others and to the organized groups and the more they agree with the conventional values, the less likely they are to break the rules.

© 2014 koya979. Used under license of Shutterstock, Inc.

Scholars who follow the **labeling theory** have a different perspective. Instead of focusing on the individual who commits the deviant behavior, they pay attention to the people who are labeling someone as deviant. They make three assumptions. No behavior is deviant until someone labels it to be deviant. Everyone commits deviant behavior at some point, such as lying or cheating. The behavior is only considered deviant in certain times in certain situations among certain people. William Chambliss (1973) studied two groups of boys in the same high school. The members of one group were upper class, while the members of the other group were poor. The frequency with which both groups of boys committed delinquent acts was similar. However, the upper-class boys never got in trouble with the law while the lower-class boys were constantly in trouble with the police. The upper-class boys had the ability to be less visible, held a demeanor that symbolized civility, and had no police bias against them. This was not the case for the lower-class boys. These boys were labeled as troublemakers so that is how everyone saw them. Once labeled as a deviant it becomes much harder to break the stereotype and much easier to meet those expectations as individuals.

The explanations for committing deviant behavior and crime involve society's cultural expectations and society's social institutions, on the one hand, and interpersonal attachments and labels, on the other hand. Consequently, the sociological explanations range from top-down to bottom-up, but all focus on the social environment in which people reside.

JOB SKILLS: Office Banter

In some places of employment, bosses and coworkers tease each other. The social atmosphere, however, can quickly turn unprofessional and even hostile. W.I. Thomas, a sociologist from the early 1900s, argued that if people define something as real, even if it is not, it is real in its consequences. This has become known as the **Thomas theorem** (Merton 1995). This idea is also similar to the propositions of labeling theory. When someone is labeled, other people may consider the label to be real. The person who is labeled may also come to believe it—a self-fulfilling prophecy. In both cases, the work and the relationships may be negatively impacted. It is best to be careful with teasing and labeling people in the workplace. Holding a respectful and professional attitude is likely to be more meaningful and effective in terms of potential for individual promotion, interoffice relations, and productive output, than other approaches.

thinking *critically*

Is there anything positive that can come out of deviant and criminal behavior?

FUNCTIONS AND DYSFUNCTIONS OF DEVIANCE

When most people think about deviance and crime, they likely believe that such behavior only has negative effects. However, deviance and crime have functions and dysfunctions. The **dysfunctions of deviance** relate to social institutions and are more intuitive. A mail carrier who throws the mail away rather than completing the route may negatively affect numerous people. A divorced father who does not pay child support harms the family and limits the development of the children. Police officers who do not patrol poorer neighborhoods may quicken the downward spiral of a community. However, deviant behavior may also have its functions. It unifies people in the attempt to stop it, such as neighbors who get together to keep the neighborhood safe. **Functions of deviance** clarify cultural norms—which ones are important, what they mean, and what the appropriate punishment should be. Lastly, it may also lead to societal change. Even an individual, such as Rosa Parks refusing to sit in the back of the bus, may spark positive change. Or, protest movements may elicit change. Some crimes may show the weaknesses in the social system, such as hackers gaining illegal information. Because deviance is based on cultural norms, it is not objective. It may lead to a better society.

SUMMARY

Deviance is a behavior that breaks cultural norms. Perceptions of deviance therefore change over time, and deviance is defined differently in different places. For example, in the United States, someone who drinks alcohol before age 21 is considered deviant. Yet, in many other countries, it is considered acceptable. Social control refers to the strategies that keep people from breaking the rules. Laws are formalized norms, which if broken, may result in a fine or prison time. The United States has a large prison population, the majority of which consists of ethnoracial minority males between the ages of 20 and 39 who have been sentenced for violent crimes. Over the years, many scholars have put

---

forward explanations about the reasons for which people engage in deviant behavior and commit crime. Currently most theories focus on the social environment. Even though most people probably see deviance as a negative behavior for society, it does have some positive functions. It brings people together, clarifies important cultural norms, and can lead to social change.

Suggested Reading:

Irwin, Katherine. 2003. "Saints and Sinners: Elite Tattoo Collectors and Tattooists as Positive and Negative Deviants." *Sociological Spectrum* 23:27-57.

ACTIVE LEARNING PROJECTS

In Class:

1. Think back to a time in your own life when you did something deviant. In writing, describe who thought it was deviant and why? Do you consider it deviant and why?
2. In a small group, discuss and write answers to the following questions: What is the extent of alcohol use in your educational institution? Have you witnessed deviance because of alcohol? What would be some solutions?
3. What the video *Spin the Bottle: Sex, Lies and Alcohol* and in a small group discuss the extent to which the information in the video is similar to your social world and the double standards for women compared to men with respect to alcohol use.
4. In a small group, list some behaviors that would be considered deviant for women but not for men and vice versa and discuss why there are differences.
5. In a small group, think of some of the ways the government uses technology to keep people from doing, or discovered that people engaged in, deviant or criminal behavior. Discuss to what extent the government should be able to control and monitor people's behaviors.

Out of Class:

1. Go to a public place or party and attempt to observe an interaction between people that is confusing or problematic. Determine whether someone was being deviant. What was the deviance, the reaction, and the consequence? How did they resolve it?
2. Find the index crimes in your state and discuss why these occur at those levels.
3. Find some controversial art (e.g., visual art, music, literature) and explore in writing why it is considered controversial.
4. Research a historical event that at the time was considered deviant or criminal but today is praised. In an essay, discuss why it was considered deviant historically but not currently.
5. Research a white-collar crime and write an essay explaining its occurrence in society using the various theories mentioned in the chapter. Critically assess how well each theory explains the behavior.

KEY TERMS

Anomie	Functions of deviance	Positive deviance
Control theory	Hate crime	Social control
Crime	Index crime	Structural strain rheory
Deviance	Informal social control	Thomas theorem
Differential association theory	Labeling theory	Victimless crime
Dysfunctions of deviance	Law	White-collar crime
Formal social control	Negative deviance	

chapter 14

Collective Behavior and
Social Movements

SOCIETAL CHANGE

Over time, societies change fundamentally in terms of social structure, behavior, and culture. Sociologists label this transformation **social change**. The cause of social change may be population growth or decline. Both large and small populations require human innovation and public policy to keep the society progressing. Human interaction with the environment also leads to change, as societies decide how to respond to different weather patterns, scarcity, and natural and manmade disasters. These processes typically change societies slowly.

War, however, can change a society fundamentally in a matter of days. From the Revolutionary War that began in 1775 to the U.S. war in Afghanistan, a 30-year period has not passed without the United States engaging in a major war. In fact, no decade has passed without the occurrence of significant U.S. military operations against another country or group of people. Some of the transformative wars in U.S. history are the Civil War, World War II, and the Vietnam War. Not only were thousands of lives lost during these wars—an enormous emotional cost in and of itself—but the United States also changed its policies and economies in response to the situations. One policy example is the Servicemen's Readjustment Act of 1944, better known as the G.I. Bill. This bill helped returning veterans with home mortgages, tuition for a college education, low-interest rate loans for businesses, and unemployment compensation. Almost 9 million veterans used the G.I. Bill. Yet, its influence spread much farther and longer than the lives of the individual service members. Their family and communities benefited. Their human capital, employment, and monetary purchases helped stimulate the U.S. economy for decades. The G.I. Bill also sparked similar bills that help military personnel today.

The Vietnam War also changed society, particularly with respect to cultural values and norms. Collective action and social movements emerged in response to the war, both in support of it and against it. The United States entered a cultural debate during and after the Vietnam War, especially with respect to how to treat military personnel as well as civilians caught in the midst of war. The emotions and cultural ideologies of the time still run deep with much of American society today. At the same time, the United States has completely transformed other societies through war, such as in Iraq and Afghanistan. The social structure, behaviors, and cultures of these two societies in particular are currently undergoing significant transformations because of the United States, regardless of the individual choices and desires of the majority of the people in those countries. Both pro-war and anti-war arguments can be made. In either case, since the nation's beginning in 1776, around 235 years ago, the United States has used its armed forces over 200 times to change or help change the societies of other countries, for better or worse (Pei and Kasper 2003).

Technological innovation also changes society. It may give rise to new products and services or ideas and policies. The printing press, the cotton-gin, the automobile, the airplane, the nuclear bomb, and television are all examples of technological innovations that have changed societies. In recent times, the computer has had a tremendous transformational effect on the United States. During the 1970s and 1980s, the country changed from a manufacturing-based economy to a service-based economy, in large part due to the computer. The effect was that many groups lost their jobs as the manufacturing sector shrank and more people entered higher education to gain the knowledge necessary for the growing service sector. The majority of U.S. occupations today exist in the service sector. Yet, all occupations are influenced by the computer, from farming and factory work to finance and federal jobs. At the same time, the computer has greatly facilitated the spread of culture throughout the world. People who are living thousands of miles away may communicate verbally and visually in real-time with each other through a personal computer. The mass media in particular have taken advantage of this innovation to report global events.

"He is a Creature of the Web. He must log on to survive."

© 2014 Cartoonresource. Used under license of Shutterstock, Inc.

Technological innovation enables **cultural diffusion**, which is the process of spreading cultural values, norms, and beliefs across groups and societies. The combination of technological innovation and cultural diffusion may spur large-scale social change. For example, Harlow (2011) documents a social movement in Guatemala that began online, mainly through the social media sites of Facebook and YouTube, and moved to offline protests. She says that within three days after their creation, the Facebook protest pages gained 28,000 friends, and that not long afterward organizers were able to gather over 50,000 people to demonstrate for weeks in downtown Guatemala City against government violence in the country. Arguably, much of the strength of the Arab Spring has been due to technological innovations, such as cell phones and the Internet, and the spread of democratic cultural values, transforming many societies in the Middle East.

CHECK POINT: What is social change and why does it happen?

COLLECTIVE BEHAVIOR

Collective behavior refers to the occurrence of a large number of people who spontaneously think and act in a similar way. The potential examples are vast, from concert goers giving a standing ovation to community members rioting in the streets. But collective behavior can be categorized into different types of action. An important point is that often the social context may constrain or ease the degree of collective behavior. In a society where there is a great amount of socioeconomic inequality, there may be more emergence of collective behavior. Furthermore, some physical locations are more conducive to collective behavior than other places, particularly ones that have comparatively open spaces so that people may interact.

Mass hysteria and **panic** represent similar types of collective behavior. People may be frightened by an unknown or unfamiliar force, leading them to respond in similarly anxious ways. The 1938 radio broadcast of *The War of the Worlds,* which has a plot where aliens from Mars attack people on earth, upset a number of listeners because they believed that the broadcast was a news report rather than a drama. Orson Welles, who ran the program, received many panicked and angry calls afterward. Yet, at the same time, the response brought him immediate national fame. Other occurrences of mass hysteria or panics have included reactions to beliefs about the presence of toxic gas, poisoned fruit, dangerous bugs, and roaming serial killers, resulting in many people developing physical and mental symptoms even though none of the rumors or stories was true.

A **crowd** is another form of collective behavior. It consists mostly of strangers in a close physical proximity to each other. One type of crowd is called a *casual crowd,* where people gather to see, hear, taste, or smell something. These crowds may emerge in front of store windows, in parks or food courts. They are a collection of people grouped together to do something similar, but they have little else in common. A *conventional crowd* represents a gathering with more purpose and often has norms to guide behavior. People who attend a monster truck show know where to go and what to do during their time together. For instance, running onto the track would be violating a norm. An *expressive crowd* refers to a group of strangers who congregate in a place for some personal gratification based on being together rather than focusing on some object in order to express an emotion. This may involve singing or dancing or some other expressive behavior. They may be religious or secular. For instance, many people attend religious meetings or education camps. Lastly, there is the *acting crowd*, which comes together with the purpose of achieving some goal. Riots and protesting are more examples. Contagion theory argues that the crowd can take on a life of its own as strangers come together and forgo responsibility for the situation and any pertinent norms and are swept up by the emotions of the moment, such as seen in instances of looting.

Social Movements

Social movements are an organized collection of people who attempt to bring about some type of specific change or to resist a specific change within a society. The topic of interest varies widely, ranging from cultural ideologies to social structural inequalities. Social movements may work on behalf of animals, the environment, or people. The type of social movement also varies widely. There are **regressive movements** that want to bring society back to an earlier state of being. There are **reformist movements** that attempt to change some institutional characteristic in order to prevent something from happening, such as an animal extinction, or to encourage something to happen, such as educational freedom for women. There are also **revolutionary** and **counterrevolutionary movements** that seek to either make fundamental changes to a society in terms of political, economic, or social structures, or to keep the current social order. The primary objective in all types of social movements is to directly take action in order to realize change rather than using indirect action or waiting for change to emerge organically.

In general, social movements go through four stages. They emerge with a few people identifying a particular topic and communicating the need for action. Then, there is a coalescence of people through organized meetings and demonstrations where the movement's values and beliefs are privately and publically expressed. Following this, the movement becomes formalized with established statuses and organizational policies that attempt to widen the movement's impact through publicity, recruitment of new members, and political change. Lastly, the movement declines. It may lack funding, the primary problem may be solved, the public interest may dwindle, or it may be absorbed into another movement. In the United States, there are currently over 100 social movements.

thinking *critically*

Why do social movements emerge in society?

Social Movement Theory

Scholars theorize about each aspect of a social movement's life. One reason a social movement emerges is because a group of people feels deprived. The deprivation can be objective. Some people may not have enough education, for example, and believe that the costs to attain education are too high. Or, the deprivation may be relative. People may believe that others have an unfair advantage. The Occupy Wall Street movement is an example of a social movement that emerged based on ideas of relative deprivation. **New social movement theories** argue that social movements emerge and people stay involved because of a combination of cultural ideologies and personal identity. **Resource mobilization theory** changes the focus from individuals to the organizational structure of the social movements. The organizational structure may include material necessities, such as money and volunteers, and nontangible services, such as the degree of personal morals and prior experience. These things facilitate the extent to which the social movement can acquire new members and keep the members, or explain the eventual decline and death of a social movement. There are many layers to social movements, including the individual, the group, and the society in which the social movement is active.

JOB SKILLS: Resumes and Cover Letters

One way to make societal changes is to start with the individual. When people change themselves, society changes in response. For example, as more individuals find work, the whole country benefits, such as through tax revenue and economic progress. In terms of employment, employers take resumes and cover letters seriously. They have limited amounts of time and need to get a sense of a potential employee quickly. The resume and cover letter should look professional and read well. Search the Internet for examples and have someone check them over before sending them to future employers. Also, realize that different occupations are interested in different knowledge and abilities. If you apply to different jobs, focus your resume and cover letter to highlight your knowledge and skills pertinent to those particular employers' interests.

SUMMARY

A society experiences social change when its social structures, behavioral patterns, and culture transform significantly. Some of the social dynamics that may be functions of social change include population processes, interactions with the environment, war, technological advancements, and cultural diffusion. People may also congregate and engage in collective behavior, from mass hysteria and panic to casual and active crowds. A social movement is an organized effort by a collection of people to change a specific part of society. There are many types of social movements, from reformist to revolutionary, but all go through a life cycle of emergence, coalescence, formalization, and decline. Scholars theorize that social movements emerge, grow, and decline because of societal deprivation, ideology, and resource mobilization dynamics. Lastly, as each individual changes oneself, such as gaining a higher education, the society, which by definition is composed of individuals, will change as well.

Suggested Reading:

Harlow, Summer. 2012. "Social Media and Social Movements: Facebook and an Online Guatemalan Justice Movement that Moved Offline." *New Media and Society* 14:225-243.

ACTIVE LEARNING PROJECTS ⎯⎯⎯⎯⎯⎯⎯⎯⎯⎯⎯⎯⎯⎯⎯

In Class:

1. Write an answer to the following question: If you could change one thing about society, what would it be and why?
2. Write about a time when you were a part of a crowd and did things that you did not think that you would do. What were your feelings at the time? Why did you behave that way? Would you do it again? Why or why not?
3. Pick a social problem that you think needs solving and create a flyer to attract people to a meeting or discussion about it.
4. In a small group, discuss how many social media sites you are a part of and to what extent it affects your feelings and decisions and why.
5. In a small group, discuss what social movement events you have participated in and how and why you got involved. If you have not participated in any social movement events, discuss what would be something that would make you get involved.

Out of Class:

1. Using the Internet, identify a social movement and describe its organizational characteristics and goals. Offer some ideas on how it might improve itself.
2. Go to a university club or organization, such as the Women's Center, and find out about their organization—how they got started, what they do to stay funded, how they recruit, how they help people, and other characteristics.
3. Research about a time in the last two years when a group of people experienced mass panic or mass hysteria. Write about the details and offer a judgment on why it happened.
4. Research some art of current social movements. What are the similarities and the differences? Speculate why the social movement or group chose that type of art to make its point.
5. Interview someone who gave time in a social movement, asking about their experiences, opinions, regrets, advice, and hopes.

KEY TERMS

Collective behavior	Mass hysteria	Resource mobilization theory
Counterrevolutionary movements	New social movement theories	Revolutionary movements
Crowd	Panic	Social change
Cultural diffusion	Reformist movements	Social movement
	Regressive movements	

appendix

Careers for Sociology Graduates

The number of undergraduate students graduating in sociology has steadily increased since the mid-1980s, reaching approximately 29,000 degrees awarded in 2010 (American Sociological Association 2013). This number equates to approximately 2 percent of all bachelor degrees awarded in that year (U.S. Department of Education 2012). There tend to be more sociology majors than economics majors but fewer than political science, psychology, and especially business majors. One reason for the differences may be that the curriculum of sociology programs typically focuses on content, method, and theory more than on particular occupational skills. The sociology major is designed to endow students with a range of skills—such as being able to solve problems through critical thinking and through effective communication—rather than to train students for specific occupations.

This strategy has its costs and benefits. On the negative side, students who graduate with a sociology major tend to have lower salaries than other students. Out of 130 majors, it ranks 100 with respect to postgraduate earnings. In 2013, the median starting salary for a sociology graduate was $36,000 and the median midcareer salary was $56,700 (PayScale.com 2013). Although not particularly high, the starting salary in sociology is comparable to a host of other popular majors, including education, journalism, zoology, anthropology, graphic design, criminal justice, psychology, and public health, among others. In terms of midcareer salaries, sociology is comparable to the disciplines of broadcasting, health care administration, dietetics, interior design, theater, and horticulture, among others.

It is also worthwhile to note that only 27 percent of all college graduates are currently employed in a job that matches their college major (Plumer 2013). Defined differently, 60 percent of college graduates are unable to find full-time employment in their field of study (Crotty 2012). This suggests that developing skills during college that are transferable to a wide range of potential jobs can be advantageous. Spalter-Roth and colleagues (2010) surveyed more than 1,500 sociology graduates over a 4-year time frame. They found that about 70 percent of these students said they learned about critical views of society, social issues, and the relationship between individuals and social institutions . Furthermore, over 70 percent of them also said that they learned to develop evidence-based arguments, to evaluate methods, and write reports. On the positive side, therefore, sociology majors come away with skills that most employers will want in an employee. For instance, the Association of American Colleges and Universities and the Chronicle of Higher Education ran surveys of employers. They found that the number-one trend among employers was hiring a candidate that could "think critically, communicate clearly and solve complex problems" regardless of the candidate's undergraduate major (Sternberg 2013:1). Only 19 percent of employers said that they look for a candidate with a specific college major. With a sociology major, the range of possible job opportunities is great.

Sociology graduates work in a variety of occupations. Based on survey research, the largest percentage of sociology graduates work in social service and counseling occupations for nonprofit organizations (Spalter-Roth et al. 2010). Some of the corresponding jobs help domestic violence victims, the poor, adolescents, migrants, and parolees. The following are examples: Americorp volunteer, caseworker for HIV-positive individuals, meals-on-wheels worker, forensic interviewer, manager of self-learning programs, migrant recruiter, and advocate for victims of domestic violence and child abuse. Other sociology graduates work in positions of administrative support, from information technology to human resources to employee training programs. Another group of sociology graduates found work with local governments, including jobs as teachers, librarians, police officers, and crime scene investigators.

A large percentage of sociology graduates also further their education with a master of arts or doctoral degree. After graduating with a master of arts degree in sociology, individuals are most likely to work for a state government agency. Over 30 percent of the graduates are also likely to use their applied research skills, which was a surprise to them (van Vooren and Spalter-Roth 2011). Many sociology majors find work with opinion polling firms and public affairs companies, especially when they have an emphasis in statistics or research methods. Over 80 percent of individuals who graduate with a doctoral degree in sociology find work in academia, teaching and doing research. The other 20 percent tend to work in the private sector or for nonprofit organizations, such as consulting firms, community action networks, and foundations. The median salary for individuals who obtained a master's degree or doctorate in sociology was $72,360 in 2010 (Bureau of Labor Statistics 2012c). The growth rate for sociology jobs over the next 10 years is expected to be 18 percent, which is about the same as the national growth rate for all occupations.

At any level, there are job opportunities for sociology graduates. Although the wages and salaries may be on the lower end of the spectrum, unless a postgraduate degree is obtained, the range of potential occupations may be comparatively greater. In a labor market environment where the average job is held for only 4.4 years (Meister 2012), having transferable skills from a sociology degree may be quite valuable and rewarding.

glossary

A

Achieved status: A social position someone has worked for.

Activity theory: A theory of aging that states that people desire to be active and have social companionship throughout all life stages rather than wanting to disengage from society.

Age integration theory: A theory of aging that argues that social institutions are segregated or integrated by age, which affects the extent to which people are able to participate in society.

Agents of socialization: Social structural entities in society that teach people the values, norms, and beliefs of society.

Aggregate: A collection of people who are in the same place at the same time.

Aging: The process of growing older biologically and passing through a number of socially constructed life course stages and relationships.

Anomie: A state when people in the group or population are unaware of, or unclear about, the cultural norms, or see the cultural norms as having weak sanctions.

Ascribed status: A social position someone has been given by society.

B

Between-group variation: A measurement of distance—or amount of variation—between two groups in regards to a particular characteristic.

Biological perspective: An explanation that sees the similarities and differences between people as originating from biological characteristics.

Biology theories of aging: Theories of aging that focus on the biological processes of the human body to explain why people grow older.

Black-White gap: The socioeconomic difference between Whites and Blacks.

Bourgeois: Capitalists who own the means of production.

Bureaucracy: The hierarchal structures that have specific lines of authority, overt rules, and procedures for how to carry out daily tasks, of formal organizations.

C

Category: A collection of people who share some social characteristic but are otherwise unrelated.

Chronological aging: The numeric, time-dependent conception of aging.

Class: A collection of people who have similar opportunities to achieve economic advancement, especially with respect to their comparable levels of education, occupational prestige, and income or wealth.

Climate change: A transformation in global temperature and weather patterns.

Closed stratification system: A social structure that limits a person's ability to achieve the desirable resources in a society because of an ascribed status.

Coding: The process of organizing data into meaningful categories that can be logically linked together and easily accessible.

Cognitive development theory: A theory that argues that children are not only passive receivers of culture expectations of gender but also seek out gender identities and roles.

Collective behavior: The process of a large number of people who spontaneously think and act in a similar way.

Complete observer: A method of collecting data where the researcher refrains from doing any of the activities and just watches the participants.

Complete participant: A method of collecting data where the researcher does whatever the participants under observation are doing.

Control theory: A theory of deviance that states that people are less likely to engage in deviant behavior when they have emotional attachments to others, have ties to formal groups in society, have commitments to the formal groups, and hold conventional values.

Control variable: A variable that is held constant when examining a relationship of interest.

Convenient sample: A collection of people that were gathered unsystematically by a researcher.

Countercultures: Groups of people that share cultural norms, values, and beliefs that are perceived by the larger society or at least by the powerful groups in the larger society to be at odds with the dominant culture or threatening in some way.

Counterrevolutionary movement: A social movement that seeks to keep the current social order.

Crime: A violation of law that has some degree of penalty.

Critical gerontology approach: A theoretical framework of aging that argues that an examination of global dynamics is necessary to understand the aging process of individuals.

Cross-sectional survey: A type of questionnaire that asks a diverse selection of people at one point in time a variety of questions.

Crowd: A collection of mostly strangers in a close physical proximity to each other.

Cultural beliefs: Shared ideas about reality.

Cultural capital: The cultural knowledge of the norms, values, beliefs, and practices of the people who can make things happen.

Cultural diffusion: The process of spreading cultural values, norms, and beliefs across groups and societies.

Cultural relativism: The idea that using another culture's perspective will aid in understanding the reasons behind that culture's behaviors without making judgments.

Cultural symbols: Physical and nonphysical objects that are endowed with meaning to represent something other than themselves.

Cultural transmission theory: A theory that argues that individuals are socialized from infancy to form a gender identity and take on gendered roles for which the caretakers believe are appropriate based on the gendered standards and expectations of the society.

Cultural values: Shared abstract ideas about what is right and wrong or good and bad.

Culture: The totality of values, norms, beliefs, and symbols that is associated with certain people.

Culture of poverty: A theory that states that poor people have a different set of values, norms, beliefs, and social practices that are not necessarily immoral or wrong but do not allow poor people to be economically competitive in modern times.

Culture shock: The feeling of puzzlement and surprise that comes from experiencing a new and unfamiliar culture.

Cumulative disadvantage: The process of the negative effects of multiple forms of inequality or oppression adding up over time to create greater disadvantage for a person or group of people.

D

Definition of the situation: A person's understanding of the social context as being filled with certain norms, values, symbols, and interpersonal connections.

Demographic transition theory: A theory that explains a country's change in population size by focusing on the country's transformation from being less developed to more developed in four stages.

Demography: The scientific study of the processes of fertility, mortality, and immigration to better understand the population components of size, composition, and density.

Dependent variable: The variable that is affected by something else, or the effect variable.

Deviance: Any action that violates the behavioral expectations of a group or society.

Differential association theory: A theory of deviance that argues that people learn to be deviant by interacting with other people who are acting in deviant ways.

Discrimination: The action of denying an individual or group of people material goods or opportunities based on a categorical status.

Disengagement theory: A theory of aging that argues that people typically disengage from society by changing roles and cutting of social ties.

Dramaturgical approach: A theoretical framework that argues that people behave in a certain context and in front of a certain audience based on their role at the moment.

Dysfunction: A process, typically at the institutional level, that may hinder the progress of a social system.

Dysfunctions of deviance: Negative deviance that disrupts the progress of a part or all of a social system.

E

Ecological footprint: A measure for estimating the impact humans have on the natural environment.

Ecology: The study of organisms interacting with the natural environment.

Emerging adulthood: A period in the life course that is after adolescence but before adulthood.

Environmental justice: The equal treatment and involvement of all people regardless of social status with respect to realizing the protection of environmental laws and experiencing a safe natural environment.

Environmental racism/discrimination: The attitudes and behaviors of the majority group with respect to placing the burden of environmental waste mainly on minority groups.

Environmental sustainability: The idea of people and industries using only the amount of environmental materials that the earth can replenish within an appropriate time to support human life indefinitely.

Ethnicity: A set of socially constructed categories in which people place themselves and others based on perceived cultural traits.

Ethnocentrism: The act of assuming one's own culture is superior and the standard by which other cultures should be judged.

Exchange theory: A theory that argues that people engage in exchange relationships with each other to maximize their benefits and reduce their costs.

F

Family: A powerful primary group.

Fecundity: The biological capacity of having children.

Feminist perspective: A framework that argues for equality between men and women in society's social institutions.

Fertility: The behavior of having children.

Field notes: All of the information that the researcher writes down from observations and interviews in location of study.

Folkways: A type of norm that has the weakest sanctions.

Formal organization: Intentionally designed entities that have an official system of operation for the purpose of achieving an overt objective.

Formal social control: The control strategies that have been institutionalized and are performed by persons in authority.

Functional aging: The objective actions a person can accomplish and the subjective perceptions of how a person looks.

Functions of deviance: To clarify cultural norms—which ones are important, what they mean, and what the appropriate punishment should be.

G

Gender: The sociocultural symbols, characteristics, and behaviors that society ascribes to men and women.

Gender identity: Personal conceptions of what it means to be a male or a female.

Gender inequality: The situation where one gender has more or less of the society's resources than another gender.

Gender role: Society-ascribed and culturally expected behaviors for a man and a woman.

Gender socialization: The concept in which both men and women are socialized to believe that each gender has certain attributes that make a person better or worse at something.

Generalized other: The perceived expectations, attitudes, and viewpoints of the whole community.

Global inequality: The situation where one country has more or less of the world's resources than another country.

Group: Two or more people who share similar cultural traits, participate in similar social practices, and typically have a feeling of affinity for one another.

H

Hate crime: A criminal action against someone or someone's property based on bias against the person's race, religion, disability, ethnic/national origin, sexual orientation, or some other official status.

Hawthorne effect: The occurrence of people changing their viewpoints and actions when they believe that someone is watching them or when they believe that they are placed in artificial circumstances.

Horizontal mobility: An individual's or group's movement from one social position to another social position within the same location in the society's stratification system.

Hypothesis: A statement about the potential relationship between two or more social constructs that is an observable and testable answer to the research question.

I

The I: A concept that represents the unique aspects of a person.

Impression management: The action of trying to present a self that pleases the audience.

Income: The amount of money people make from salaries and wages and any earnings from investments.

Independent variable: The variable that affects or predicts another variable, the causal variable.

Index crime: The main categories of crime that are reported in the Uniform Crime Reports.

Industrial Revolution: A time period in human history when there was significant change in the way things were manufactured, grown, processed, and distributed.

Informal social control: The casual techniques that get people to conform to expected behaviors.

In-group: The group of people in which a person is a member by way of relationships and emotion.

Intergenerational mobility: The changes in social positions across two or more lifetimes within the same family unit.

International migration: The transfer of people from residing in one country to residing in another country.

Interpretative sociology: A sociological approach to studying society by focusing on how individuals see and understand their social environments and behaviors.

Intersex: A category of people who have a combination of the standard biological differences between men and women.

Intragenerational mobility: The personal changes in social positions within an individual's lifetime.

L

Labeling theory: A theory used to explain deviance by focusing on what people call individuals who they believe acted inappropriately.

Latent function: The unexpected and unintended outcomes of a part of the social system.

Law: Formalized norms to control deviant behavior.

Law of Three Stages: Auguste Comte's idea that society progresses through three stages of development in terms of gaining knowledge: theological, metaphysical, and positive or scientific.

Life course perspective: A theoretical framework that explains how people age over time.

Life expectancy: The average number of years left to live at any given age.

Literature review: The process of reading as many studies as possible on a particular area of interest in order to understand the main theories, methodologies, findings, and conclusions of the topic.

Longevity: The average length of life of a person in a particular population.

Longitudinal survey: A type of questionnaire that asks the same people the same questions over a designated period of time.

Looking-glass self: A theoretical idea that people create a social identity by determining what they think other people think of them.

M

Macrosociology: A sociological approach to studying society that focuses on large-scale social systems and phenomena.

Macro theories of aging: Theories that focus on the larger structural conditions of society to explain individuals' aging process.

Manifest function: The expected and intended outcomes of a part of the social system.

Mass hysteria: A collective behavior whereby people may be frightened by an unknown or unfamiliar force, leading them to respond in similarly anxious ways.

Master status: The social status of a person that dominates all of the other statuses in the individual's mind or the minds of other people and through which the person will be evaluated in terms of what role he or she is supposed to play in society.

Material culture: All of the tangible objects that humans make and to which they give meaning.

Matrix of domination: A concept to represent the intersecting social structures of oppression that have a cumulative and negative effect on minority group members.

The Me: A concept that represents what people believe other people think of them, or the process of seeing the self as an object.

Mechanical solidarity: A type of cohesion between a collection of people that is based on social similarities and little division in labor.

Mezzo theories of aging: Theories that incorporate the idea that interactions with other people affect a person's aging process; it is not solely up to an individual.

Microsociology: A sociological approach to studying society that focuses on small-scale interpersonal dynamics and phenomena.

Micro theories of aging: Theories of aging that focus specifically on individuals.

Mix-methods: A research technique that uses both quantitative and qualitative strategies to gather data.

Morbidity: The extent of sickness in a population.

Mores: A category of norms that have moderate sanctions.

Mortality: The occurrence of death in a population.

N

Natural environment: All the physical attributes of the earth below, on top of, and above the ground, consisting of living organisms and natural materials.

Negative deviance: Behavior that counters a cultural norm.

Neoclassical economic theory: A theory that is used to explain the SES gap between men and women by arguing that women find jobs with high starting pay and less career advancement because they leave the labor force to take care of family.

New social movement theories: A set of theories that argue that social movements emerge and people stay involved because of a combination of cultural ideologies and personal identity.

Nonmaterial culture: All of the nontangible features of human life for a set of people, including values, norms, and beliefs.

Norms: Behaviors that a group or society considers to be expected and appropriate, which if violated result in a negative sanction.

O

Old age: A stage in the life span that is typically considered to begin around age 65.

Open stratification systems: A social structure of the society that has pathways that allow people to achieve desirable resources independent of their ascribed statuses.

Organic solidarity: A type of cohesion between a collection of people that is based on interdependence in terms of labor.

Out-group: The collection of people in which a person is not a member.

P

Panic: A collective behavior whereby people may be frightened by an unknown or unfamiliar force, leading them to respond in similarly anxious ways.

Participant observer: A methodological strategy of taking part in some activities but not in others with a group of people under investigation.

Party: A group of people that band together to gain social power in order to achieve a specific goal or obtain a particular resource.

Patriarchal social system: A social system that gives more power to men than to women in consequential social institutions.

Personal trouble: The unique characteristics of the individual, in particular the characteristics that restrict the individual from succeeding.

Population policies: A set of formal rules that attempt to change a society's population in terms of size, composition, or density.

Positive deviance: Behavior that over-conforms to a norm.

Positivism: A philosophy that suggests that valid knowledge must come through the testing of observable data.

Poverty: A state of economic existence that falls below an official income line.

Power: The ability to achieve desired goals despite the opposition of others.

Prejudice: Negative opinions, beliefs, and emotions toward a group or category of people.

Presentation of self: The process of people attempting to appear a certain way by using symbols and gestures.

Primary group: A comparatively small collection of people that have long-lasting and intimate ties with one another.

Proletariat: Workers who do not own the means of production in a class system.

Psychological perspective: An explanation that sees the similarities and differences between people as originating from socio-emotional factors and immediate social environmental conditions.

Public issue: Individual and group problems that are a function of broader social structures in society.

Q

Qualitative methods: A strategy of collecting data which are based on observations and need interpretative techniques for analyses in order to understand the social life of a relatively small group of people.

Quantitative methods: A strategy of collecting data that are mainly numeric in form and need statistical techniques for analyses in order to represent a population of people.

R

Race: A set of socially constructed categories in which people place themselves and others based on perceived biological distinctions.

Racial and ethnic inequality: The notion that some racial and ethnic categories are given certain types and amounts of resources while other categories are limited from them or denied them.

Racial formations: The group-level process of determining the racial categories in which people can place themselves.

Racism: Prejudicial attitudes and discriminatory actions toward a racial category or categories of people.

Reference group: The group that is used as the standard of evaluation.

Reformist movement: A social movement that attempts to change some institutional characteristic in order to prevent something from happening or encourage something to happen.

Regressive movement: A social movement that wants to bring society back to an early state of being.

Research ethics: A code of behavior that sociologists follow in order to be honest in the research process and protective of their subjects' rights and dignities.

Resocialization: The process by which people are forced to take on a new social status and learn new cultural norms, values, beliefs, and practices.

Resource mobilization theory: A theory that focuses on the organizational structure of the social movements rather than individuals to understand who joins, stays, and quits the social movements.

Revolutionary movement: A social movement that seeks to fundamentally change a society in terms of the political, economic, or social structures.

Role conflict: The situation where a person holds two or more social statuses that have corresponding roles that are socially incompatible.

Role strain: The stress of having a social status that has very demanding roles.

S

Sandwich generation: A time period when people have dependent children and are also taking care of aging parents.

Scientific method: The process of collecting and analyzing data systematically so that other people can verify or refute the findings and conclusions.

Secondary group: A collection of people that have relatively impersonal ties that are typically more formal in nature to accomplish a particular objective.

Semistructured interview: A type of interview that typically has a set date and time with prearranged questions, yet the order of the questions is not strict and there is more participation in the discussion by the researcher.

Sex: The biological differences between men and women.

Sexism: The process of favoring one gender over another, typically male over female, while explaining the biased behavior with cultural scripts about the biological differences between the two sexes.

Sexual harassment: The act of making someone experience unwanted sexual attention or being made to feel that the workplace is a hostile environment because of their sex.

Simple random sampling: A sampling technique where everyone in the population has a known and equal chance of being selected for the survey.

Social change: The fundamental transformation of societies in terms of social structure, behavior, and culture.

Social conflict perspective: A theoretical framework that sees the social system as offering privileges to one group at the expense of another group, resulting in a struggle between the two groups for scarce resources.

Social construct: Something that humans define or create or produce or invent through their interactions.

Social constructionism: A theoretical framework that argues that people construct their realities through social interaction, making the meaning they give to objects and behaviors critical to understanding any topic.

Social construction of reality: The notion that people define what is real and what is not real through social interaction within social institutions.

Social control: The task of preventing deviant behavior.

Social inequality: The state in a stratification system where everyone does not receive equal types and amounts of resources.

Social institution: A set of social structures and cultural ideologies that arise to solve a societal problem.

Socialization: The process by which people learn the cultural norms, values, beliefs, and practices of the social environment in which they participate.

Social mobility: The process of moving through the stratification system.

Social movement: An organized collection of people who attempt to bring about some type of specific change or to resist that change within a society.

Social role: The behaviors people are supposed to enact when they take on a specific social status.

Social roles and aging: A perspective of aging that argues that a person's social roles influences how the person ages.

Social status: A position in the social system.

Social stratification: The state in a social system where groups and categories of people are ranked in a hierarchal manner so that they are allocated different types and amounts of resources.

Social structure: A set of interrelated social statuses that have identifiable social roles, which result in patterned behavior over time.

Society: The totality of social relations and cultures within an accepted geographic boundary.

Socioeconomic status: Similarities and differences in income and wealth, education, and occupation.

Sociological imagination: The ability to see individual circumstances as public issues, in addition to seeing them as personal troubles.

Sociological perspective: An explanation of human behavior that focuses on the intricacies of a social environment in which people reside.

Sociology: A scientific discipline that describes and explains human perceptions and behaviors.

Spurious relationship: The idea that a relationship is not causal because a third variable is causing both of the variables in the relationship.

Status: One of three general dimensions of social stratification and inequality, as defined by Max Weber, involving a person's level of honor or prestige.

Status inconsistency: A person who holds two or more social statuses that are at odds with each other based on social expectations.

Structural functionalist perspective: A theoretical perspective that sees society as a social system of interconnected social institutions, which have separate functions to help society survive over time.

Structured interview: A planned interview that has a specific time and place and the questions are arranged and asked in a precise order.

Structural strain theory: A theory of deviance that focuses on the mismatch between society's achievement expectations and its available means of achievement.

Subculture: A group of people that have specific cultural norms, values, and beliefs that are different or more intense from the rest of society but not counter to society.

Subjective aging: The idea that people understand their age in terms of how they feel.

Sui generis: A Latin phrase that indicates something has its own unique qualities.

Surveys: A method of collecting quantitative data by having people answer prearranged questions with specific response categories.

Symbolic interactionist perspective: A theoretical perspective that examines and explains human behavior by focusing on the meaning making and symbolic interpretations that individuals engage in during interaction.

Symbols: See *Cultural symbols*.

T

Taboos: A type of norm with the harshest sanctions.

Taxonomies: A methodological strategy of grouping people together based on shared characteristics, which can range from specific to general.

Theoretical perspective: A theoretical framework that presents a unique view of how the social world works.

Theories of migration: Push and pull factors that explain international migration.

Theory: A set of interconnected statements that explains the reason for an observed pattern of social behavior.

Thick descriptions: A strategy in qualitative methodology to describe in detail the social situation and relationships.

Thomas theorem: A theoretical idea that suggests that if people define something as real, even if it is not, it is real in its consequences.

Total institution: Organizations that separate people out from society and engage in powerful, formalized tactics of socialization.

Transgender: A state of gender identity where a person has the assigned biological features of one sex but feels like another sex.

Transition to adulthood: A period in the life course when adolescents move into adulthood biologically, psychologically, and socially.

Transsexual: The condition of changing sexual categories to align with psychological feelings through a transformation in appearance and activities, and in some cases through sex reassignment surgery.

Triangulation: The strategy of using different research methods to collect data on a single topic.

Two-sex category system: The government's system of laws that is set up for only two sex options.

Typologies: Conceptual labels for people or activities that have similar characteristics, but do not range from specific to general and do not need to completely match empirical observation.

U

Unstructured interview: A casual conversation with a member or members of the group under observation that has no prearranged questions.

V

Variable: A social construct that has a range of measurable values or characteristics and that can influence something else or be influenced by something else.

Verstehen: A German word that in English has come to represent the method of understanding behavior by learning how individuals interpret their own actions.

Vertical mobility: An individual's or group's movement up or down the society's stratification system.

Victimless crime: A type of crime where an individual commits illegal actions that do not directly affect someone else or that reflect an illegal exchange between two willing parties.

W

Wealth: The totality of economic assets that someone owns, minus any debts.

White-collar crime: A type of crime that is usually committed by business professionals or government workers who engage in fraud or run scams.

Within-group variation: A measurement of distance—or amount of variation—among members of the same group in regards to a particular characteristic.

references

Abma, Joyce, Gladys Martinez, and Casey Copen. 2010. "Teenagers in the United States: Sexual Activity, Contraceptive Use, and Childbearing: National Survey of Family Growth, 2006–2008." National Center for Health Statistics 23:1-57.

American Sociological Association. 2013. *Sociology Degrees Awarded by Degree Level.* Retrieved July 28, 2013 at http://www.asanet.org/research/stats/degrees/degrees_level.cfm

Anderson, Elijah. 1999. *The Code of the Street: Decency, Violence, and the Moral Life of the Inner City.* New York: Norton.

Appelrouth, Scott, and Laura Desfor Edles. 2008. *Classical and Contemporary Sociological Theory: Text and Readings.* Thousand Oaks, CA: Pine Forge Press.

Arnett, Jeffrey Jensen. 2000. "Emerging Adulthood: A Theory of Development from the Late Teens through the Twenties." *American Psychologist*, May: 469-480.

Axtman, Kris. 2005. "How Enron Awards Do, or Don't, Trickle Down." *The Christian Science Monitor*, June 20. Retrieved July 25, 2013 at http://www.csmonitor.com/2005/0620/p02s01-usju.html

Bailey, Carol A. 2007. *A Guide to Qualitative Field Research*. 2nd Edition. Thousand Oaks, CA: Pine Forge Press.

Barrett, Lisa Feldman, Batja Mesquita, Kevin N. Ochsner, and James J. Gross. 2007. "The Experience of Emotion." *Annual Review of Psychology* 58:373-403.

Berger, Peter L., and Thomas Luckmann. 1966. *The Social Construction of Reality: A Treatise in the Sociology of Knowledge*. New York: Anchor Books.

Blumer, Herbert. 1958. "Race Prejudice as a Sense of Group Position." *Pacific Sociological Review* 1:3-7.

Bonilla-Silva, Eduardo. 2006. *Racism Without Racists: Color-Blind Racism and the Persistence of Racial Inequality in America*. Lanham, MD: Rowman and Littlefield Publishers.

Brindis, Claire D. 2006. "A Public Health Success: Understanding Policy Changes Related to Teen Sexual Activity and Pregnancy." *Annual Review of Public Health* 27:277-295.

Brizendine, Louann. 2011. *The Male Brain*. New York: Three Rivers Press.

Bronson, Po. 2007. "How Not to Talk to Your Kids: The Inverse Power of Praise." *New York Magazine News and Features*, August 3. Retrieved July 12, 2013 at http://nymag.com/news/features/27840/

Buchen, Lizzie. 2012. "Biology and Ideology: The Anatomy of Politics." *Nature*, October 24. Retrieved July 12, 2013 at http://www.nature.com/news/biology-and-ideology-the-anatomy-of-politics-1.11645

Bureau of Labor Statistics. 2012a. May 2012 National Occupational Employment and Wage Estimates, United States. Bureau of Labor Statistics, United States Department of Labor. Retrieved July 15, 2013 at http://www.bls.gov/oes/current/oes_nat.htm

_____. 2012b. Table 11: Employed Persons by Detailed Occupation, Sex, Race, and Hispanic or Latino Ethnicity. Annual Averages. Retrieved July 19, 2013 at http://www.bls.gov/cps/cpsaat11.pdf

_____. 2012c. Occupational Outlook Handbook, Sociologists. Retrieved July 28, 2013 at http://www.bls.gov/ooh/life-physical-and-social-science/sociologists.htm

Carson, E. Ann, and William J. Sabol. 2012. "Prisoners in 2011." U.S. Department of Justice. Retrieved July 25, 2013 at http://www.bjs.gov/content/pub/pdf/p11.pdf

Censky, Annalyn. 2012. "Americans Make Up Half of the World's Richest 1%." CNN Money, January 4. Retrieved July 15, 2013 at http://money.cnn.com/2012/01/04/news/economy/world_richest/index.htm

Centers for Disease Control. 2013. *Heart Disease Facts*. Retrieved July 22, 2013 at http://www.cdc.gov/heartdisease/facts.htm

Central Intelligence Agency. 2013. *The World Factbook.* Retrieved July 22, 2013 at https://www.cia.gov/library/publications/the-world-factbook/rankorder/2102rank.html

Ceobanu, Alin M., and Xavier Escandell. 2010. "Comparative Analyses of Public Attitudes toward Immigrants and Immigration using Multinational Survey Data: A Review of Theories and Research." *Annual Review of Sociology* 36:15.1-15.20.

Chambliss, William J. 1973. "The Saints and the Roughnecks." *Society* 11:24-31.

Chandy, Laurence, and Geoffrey Gertz. 2011. "Poverty in Numbers: The Changing State of Global Poverty from 2005 to 2015." The Brookings Institution, pp. 1-23. Retrieved July 22, 2013 at http://www.brookings.edu/~/media/research/files/papers/2011/1/global%20poverty%20chandy/01_global_poverty_chandy.pdf

Christie, Les. 2012. "More than 30% of Mortgage Borrowers still Underwater." CNN Money, May 24. Retrieved July 15, 2013 at http://money.cnn.com/2012/05/24/real_estate/underwater-mortgages/index.htm

Cohn, D'Vera. 2010. "Race and the Census: The 'Negro' Controversy." Pew Research, January 21. Retrieved July 16, 2013 at http://www.pewsocialtrends.org/2010/01/21/race-and-the-census-the-%E2%80%9Cnegro%E2%80%9D-controversy/

Collins, Patricia Hill. 2000. *Black Feminist Thought: Knowledge, Consciousness, and the Politics of Empowerment.* 2nd Edition. New York: Routledge.

Condry, John, and Sandra Condry. 1976. "Sex Differences: A Study in the Eye of the Beholder." *Child Development* 47:812-819.

Crotty, James Marshall. 2012. "60% of College Grads Can't Find Work in Their Field. Is A Management Degree the Answer?" *Forbes Magazine*, March 1. Retrieved July 28, 2013 at http://www.forbes.com/sites/jamesmarshallcrotty/2012/03/01/most-college-grads-cant-find-work-in-their-field-is-a-management-degree-the-answer/

Darwin, Charles. 2003 [1859]. *The Origin of Species.* New York: Signet Classics.

Davis, Kingsley, and Wilbert E. Moore. 1945. "Some Principle of Stratification." *American Sociological Review* 10:242-249.

DeNavas-Walt, Carmen, Bernadette D. Proctor, and Jessica C. Smith. 2012. "Income, Poverty, and Health Insurance Coverage in the United States: 2011." Current Population Reports, United States Census. September. Retrieved July 15, 2013 at http://www.census.gov/prod/2012pubs/p60-243.pdf

Dickens, Charles. 1998. *A Tale of Two Cities.* Mineola, NY: Dover Publications.

Digman, John M. 1990. "Personality Structure: Emergence of the Five-Factor Model." *Annual Review of Psychology* 41:417-440.

Domhoff, G. William. 2013. *Who Rules America? Wealth, Income, and Power.* Retrieved July 15, 2013 at http://www2.ucsc.edu/whorulesamerica/power/wealth.html

Dreger, Alice Domurat. 1998. "'Ambiguous Sex'—or Ambivalent Medicine?" *The Hastings Center Report* 28:24-35.

Duhigg, Charles. 2012. "How Companies Learn Your Secrets." *The New York Times*, February 16, p. 1. Retrieved July 5, 2012 at http://www.nytimes.com/2012/02/19/magazine/shopping-habits.html?pagewanted=all

Durkheim, Emile. 1997. *Suicide: A Study in Sociology*. Translated by John A. Spaulding and George Simpson. New York: The Free Press.

Eitzen, D. Stanley. 1999. *Fair and Foul: Beyond the Myths and Paradoxes of Sport*. Lanham, MD: Rowman and Littlefield Publishers.

Elder, Todd E. 2010. "The Importance of Relative Standards in ADHD Diagnoses: Evidence Based on Exact Birth Dates." *Journal of Health Economics* 29:641-656.

Federal Bureau of Investigation. 2011. Financial Crimes Report to the Public: Fiscal Years 2010-2011. Reports and Publications. Retrieved July 25, 2013 at http://www.fbi.gov/stats-services/publications/financial-crimes-report-2010-2011

Finn, Adharanand, Ekaterina Ochagavia, Alex Healey, and Michael Tait. 2013. "Why Are Kenyans the Best Distance Runners?" The Running Blog, July 2. Retrieved July 16, 2013 at http://www.guardian.co.uk/lifeandstyle/the-running-blog/video/2013/jul/02/kenyans-best-distance-runners-video

Fischer-Baum, Reuben. 2013. "Infographic: Is Your State's Highest-Paid Employee a Coach? (Probably)." Deadspin, May 9. Retrieved July 15 at http://deadspin.com/infographic-is-your-states-highest-paid-employee-a-co-489635228

Frankfort-Nachmias, Chava, and Anna Leon-Guerrero. 2011. *Social Statistics for a Diverse Society*. 6th Edition. Thousand Oaks, CA: Pine Forge Press.

Fromherz, Allen. 2011. *Ibn Khaldun: Life and Times*. New York: Columbia University Press.

Furstenberg, Frank F. 1990. "Divorce and the American Family." *Annual Review of Sociology* 16:379-403.

Futrelle, David. 2012. "Closing the Chore Gap." Time Magazine, December 21. Retrieved July 15, 2013 at http://business.time.com/2012/12/21/closing-the-chore-gap/

Gladwell, Malcolm. 2008. *Outliers: The Story of Success*. New York: Little, Brown and Company.

Gleitman, Henry, Alan J. Fridlund, and Daniel Roisberg. 2000. *Basic Psychology*. New York: W.W. Norton & Company.

Global Footprint Network. 2013. *World Footprint*. Retrieved July 23, 2013 at http://www.footprintnetwork.org/en/index.php/GFN/page/world_footprint/

Greenstone, Michael, Adam Looney, Jeremy Patashnik, and Muxin Yu. 2013. "Thirteen Economic Facts about Social Mobility and the Role of Education." Brookings Institution, June Report. Retrieved July 15, 2013 at http://www.brookings.edu/research/reports/2013/06/13-facts-higher-education

Groves, Nancy. 2008. "From Past to Present: the Changing Demographics of Women in Medicine." American Academy of Ophthalmology. http://www.aao.org/yo/newsletter/200806/article04.cfm

Harlow, Summer. 2011. "Social Media and Social Movements: Facebook and an Online Guatemalan Justice Movement that Moved Offline." *New Media and Society* 14:225-243.

Heine, Steven J., and Emma E. Buchtel. 2009. "Personality: The Universal and the Culturally Specific." *Annual Review of Psychology* 60:369-394.

Hickey, Walter. 2013. "22 Maps that Show How Americans Speak English Totally Differently from Each Other." Retrieved July 11, 2013 from http://www.businessinsider.com/22-maps-that-show-the-deepest-linguistic-conflicts-in-america-2013-6?op=1

Hochschild, Arlie Russell. 2001. "The Nanny Chain." *The American Prospect* 11:1-4

Human Rights First. 2013. Hate Crime Report Card—the United States. Retrieved July 24, 2013 at http://www.humanrightsfirst.org/our-work/fighting-discrimination/hate-crime-report-card/hate-crime-report-card-the-united-states/

International Organization for Migration. 2013. *Facts and Figures: Global Estimates and Trends.* Retrieved July 22, 2013 at http://www.iom.int/cms/en/sites/iom/home/about-migration/facts--figures-1.html

Jablonski, Nina G., and George Chaplin. 2000. "The Evolution of Human Skin Coloration." *Journal of Human Evolution* 39:57-106.

Jacob, James R. 1998. *The Scientific Revolution: Aspirations and Achievements, 1500–1700.* Amherst, NY: Prometheus Books.

Kanter, Rosabeth Moss. 1993. *Men and Women of the Corporation.* 2nd Edition. New York: Basic Books.

Kastle, Klaus. 2013. "The Global Village." *Nations Online Project.* Retrieved July 22, 2013 at http://www.nationsonline.org/oneworld/global-village.htm

Kay, Andrea. 2011. "What Employers Want: 5 More Skills to Cultivate." *USA Today,* May 30, p. 1. Retrieved July 5, 2012 at http://www.usatoday.com/money/jobcenter/workplace/kay/2011-05-30-skills-employers-want-part-ii_N.htm

Kim, Jeongsoo, Shelley K. Irving, and Tracy A. Loveless. 2012. "Dynamics of Economic Well-Being: Participation in Government Programs, 2004 to 2007 and 2009: Who Gets Assistance?" *Current Population Reports*, July. Retrieved July 15, 2013 at http://www.census.gov/prod/2012pubs/p70-130.pdf

Langer, Gary. 2011. "One in Four U.S. Women Reports Workplace Harassment." *ABC News*, November 16. Retrieved July 19, 2013 at http://abcnews.go.com/blogs/politics/2011/11/one-in-four-u-s-women-reports-workplace-harassment/

Leicester, John. 2013. "Lance Armstrong Considers Himself Tour de France Record-Holder Still, Believes Doping Needed to Win." *Huffington Post*, June 28. Retrieved July 24, 20123 at http://www.huffingtonpost.com/2013/06/28/lance-armstrong-tour-de-france_n_3515081.html

Leman, Kevin. 2009. *The Birth Order Book: Why You Are the Way You Are.* Grand Rapids, MI: Revell Books.

Lorenz, Kate. 2009. "5 Signs of Job Burnout…and What to Do About It." *Careerbuilder.com*, December 17. Retrieved July 14, 2003 at http://www.careerbuilder.com/Article/CB-655-The-Workplace-Five-Signs-of-Job-Burnout-and-What-to-Do-About-It/

Marger, Martin N. 2008. *Social Inequality: Patterns and Processes.* 4th Edition. New York: McGraw-Hill.

Martin, Joyce A., Brady E. Hamilton, Stephanie J. Ventura, Michelle J.K. Osterman, Elizabeth C. Wilson, and T.J. Matthews. 2012. National Vital Statistics Report. U.S. Department of Health and Human Services. August 28. Retrieved July 14, 2013 at http://www.cdc.gov/nchs/data/nvsr/nvsr61/nvsr61_01.pdf

Marx, Karl. 1979. *A Contribution of the Critique of Political Economy.* Translated by N.L. Stone. Chicago: Charles H. Kerr and Company.

Massey, Douglas S. 2001. "Residential Segregation and Neighborhood Conditions in U.S. Metropolitan Areas." Pp. 291–434 in *America Becoming: Racial Trends and Their Consequences*, Vol 1. Washington, D.C.: National Academies Press.

Massey, Douglas S., and Nancy A. Denton. 1993. *American Apartheid: Segregation and the Making of the Underclass.* Cambridge, MA: Harvard University Press.

Mears, Ashley. 2009. "Size Zero High-End Ethnic: Cultural Production and the Reproduction of Culture in Fashion Modeling." *Poetics: Journal of Empirical Research on Culture, the Media, and the Arts* 38:21-46.

Meister, Jeanne. 2012. "Job Hopping Is the 'New Normal' for Millennials: Three Ways to Prevent a Human Resource Nightmare." *Forbes Magazine*, August 14. Retrieved July 28, 2013 at http://www.forbes.com/sites/jeannemeister/2012/08/14/job-hopping-is-the-new-normal-for-millennials-three-ways-to-prevent-a-human-resource-nightmare/

Merton, Robert K. 1968. *Social Theory and Social Structure.* New York: The Free Press.

_____. 1995. "The Thomas Theorem and the Matthew Effect." *Social Forces* 74:379-424.

Milkie, Melissa A. 1999. "Social Comparisons, Reflected Appraisals, and Mass Media: The Impact of Pervasive Beauty Images on Black and White Girls' Self Concepts." *Social Psychology Quarterly* 62:190-210.

Mills, C. Wright. 2000. *The Sociological Imagination*. New York: Oxford University Press.
National Institute on Alcohol Abuse and Alcoholism. 2013. "College Drinking." Retrieved on February 7, 2014 at http://www.niaaa.nih.gov/alcohol-health/special-populations-co-occurring-disorders/college-drinking

National Institute of Environmental Health Sciences and Environmental Health Perspectives. 2010. *A Human Health Perspective on Climate Change.* Research Triangle Park, NC: Environmental Perspectives and National Institute of Environmental Health Sciences

Newton, Michael. 2004. *Savage Girls and Wild Boys: A History of Feral Children*. New York: Picador.

Olson, Samantha. 2013. "CDC Says U.S. Life Expectancy Is Up: Which State, Gender, and Race are Living Longest?" *Medical Daily*, July 18. Retrieved July 22, 2013 at http://www.medicaldaily.com/articles/17553/20130718/cdc-life-expectancy-retirement-mortality-rate-health-life-expectancy.htm

Omi, Michael, and Howard Winant. 1994. *Racial Formation in the United States from the 1960s to the 1990s*. 2nd Edition. New York: Routledge.

Pager, Devah, Bruce Western, and Bart Bonikowski. 2009. "Discrimination in a Low-Wage Labor Market: A Field Experiment." *American Sociological Review* 74:777-799.

PayScale.com. 2013. Majors that Pay You Back. Retrieved July 28, 2013 at http://www.payscale.com/college-salary-report-2013/majors-that-pay-you-back

Pei, Minxin, and Sara Kasper. 2003. "Lessons from the Past: The American Record on Nation Building." *Carnegie Endowment for International Peace*. Retrieved July 2013 at http://carnegieendowment.org/files/Policybrief24.pdf

Peterson, Ruth D., and Lauren J. Krivo. 2005. "Macrostructural Analyses of Race, Ethnicity, and Violent Crime: Recent Lessons and New Directions for Research." *Annual Review of Sociology* 31:331-356.

Pew Research Center. 2008. *High Marks for the Campaign, a High Bar for Obama*. November 13, Pp. 1–7. Retrieved July 19, 2013 at http://www.people-press.org/2008/11/13/high-marks-for-the-campaign-a-high-bar-for-obama/

Pierret, Charles R. 2006. "The 'Sandwich Generation': Women Caring for Parents and Children." *Monthly Labor Review*, September 3-9.

Plumer, Brad. 2013. "Only 27 Percent of College Grads Have a Job Related to Their Major." *The Washington Post*, May 20. Retrieved July, 28 2013 at http://www.washingtonpost.com/blogs/wonkblog/wp/2013/05/20/only-27-percent-of-college-grads-have-a-job-related-to-their-major/

Quadagno, Jull. 2011. *Aging and the Life Course: An Introduction to Social Gerontology*. 5th Edition. New York: McGraw-Hill.

Rivera, Lauren A. 2010. "Status Distinctions in Interaction: Social Selection and Exclusion at an Elite Nightclub." *Qualitative Sociology* 33:229-255.

Roediger, David R. 2005. *Working toward Whiteness: How America's Immigrants Became White*. New York: Basic Books.

Sakai, Katsuyuki. 2008. "Task Set and Prefrontal Cortex." *Annual Review of Neuroscience* 31:219-245.

Sampson, Robert J., and John H. Laub. 2003. "Desistance from Crime over the Life Course." Pp. 295-309 in *Handbook of the Life Course*, edited by Jeylan T. Mortimer and Michael J. Shanahan. New York: Kluwer Academic/Plenum Publishers.

Sanders, Clinton R. 2003. "Actions Speaker Louder than Words: Close Relationships between Humans and Nonhuman Animals." *Symbolic Interaction* 26:405-426.

Shah, Anup. 2013. "Poverty Facts and Statistics." *Global Issues: Social Political, Economic and Environmental Issues that Affect Us All*. Retrieved July 22, 2013 at http://www.globalissues.org/article/26/poverty-facts-and-stats#src4

Shively, Michael. 2005. "Study of Literature and Legislation on Hate Crime in America. *National Institute of Justice*. March 31. Retrieved July 24, 2013 at https://www.ncjrs.gov/pdffiles1/nij/grants/210300.pdf

South, Scott J., and Katherine Trent. 2010. "Imbalanced Sex Ratios, Men's Sexual Behavior, and Risk of Sexually Transmitted Infection in China." *Journal of Health and Social Behavior* 51:376-390.

Spalter-Roth, Roberta, Mary Scheuer Senter, Pamela Stone, and Michael Wood. 2010. "ASA's Bachelor's and Beyond Survey: Findings and Their Implications for Students and Departments." *Teaching Sociology* 38:314-329.

Stempel, Carl. 2006. "Gender, Social Class, and the Sporting Capital-Economic Capital Nexus." *Sociology of Sport Journal* 23:273-292.

Sternberg, Robert J. 2013. "Giving Employers What They Don't Really Want." *The Chronicle of Higher Education*, June 17. Retrieved July 28, 2013 at http://chronicle.com/article/Giving-Employers-What-They/139877/

Sutter, John. 2012. "Slavery's Last Stronghold." *CNN Freedom Project*, March 17. Retrieved July 24, 2013 at http://www.cnn.com/interactive/2012/03/world/mauritania.slaverys.last.stronghold/index.html

Taylor, Kate. 2012. "Even Women Doctors Can't Escape the Pay Gap." *Forbes Magazine*, June 13. Retrieved July 19, 2013 at http://www.forbes.com/sites/katetaylor/2012/06/13/even-women-doctors-cant-escape-the-pay-gap/

Todes, Daniel. 2000. *Ivan Pavlov: Exploring the Animal Machine*. New York: Oxford University Press.

United Nations Refugee Agency. 2011. *UNHCR Global Trends 2011: A Year in Crisis.* Retrieved July 22, 2013 at http://www.unhcr.org/4fd6f87f9.html

United States Census. 2011. International Programs. Retrieved July 20, 2013 at http://www.census.gov/population/international/data/worldpop/table_history.php and http://www.census.gov/population/international/data/idb/worldpopgraph.php

United States Department of Education. 2012. The Condition of Education 2012. Retrieved July 28, 2013 at http://nces.ed.gov/fastfacts/display.asp?id=72

United States Energy Information Administration. 2013. Frequently Asked Questions. Retrieved July 23, 2013 at http://www.eia.gov/tools/faqs/faq.cfm?id=87&t=1

United States Environmental Protection Agency. 2013. "Climate Change is Happening." Retrieved February 7, 2014 at http://www.epa.gov/climatechange/basics/#happening

Van Vooren, Nicole, and Roberta Spalter-Roth. 2011. "Sociology Master's Graduates Join the Workforce." *American Sociological Association.* Retrieved July 28, 2013 at http://www.asanet.org/research/sociology_masters_graduates_in_the_workforce.pdf

Venkates, Sudhir. 2008. *Gang Leader for a Day: A Rogue Sociologist Takes to the Streets.* New York: The Penguin Press.

Vincent, Grayson K., and Victoria A. Velkoff. 2010. "The Next Four Decades: The Older Population in the United States—2010 to 2050." U.S. Census Bureau, Pp. 1–14. Retrieved July 13, 2013 at http://www.census.gov/prod/2010pubs/p25-1138.pdf

Voss, Gretchen. 2008. "Inside the Gloucester Pregnancy Pact." *Marie Claire*, September 19, Pp. 1–3. Retrieved July 5, 2012 from http://www.marieclaire.com/world-reports/news/teenage-pregnancy-pact-gloucester-3

Weightman, Gavin. 2010. *The Industrial Revolutionaries: The Making of the Modern World 1776–1914.* New York: Grove Press.

Williams, Christine L. 1992. "The Glass Escalator: Hidden Advantages for Men in the 'Female' Professions." *Social Problems* 39:253-267.

Williams, Gregory Howard. 1996. *Life on the Color Line: The True Story of a White Boy Who Discovered He Was Black.* New York: First Plume Printing.

Wilson, William Julius. 1996. *When Work Disappears.* New York: Knopf.

Yeats, William Butler. 1996. *William Butler Yeats: Selected Poems and Four Plays.* Edited by M.L. Rosenthal. New York: Scribner.

subject index

A

Cooley, Charles Horton, 45, 81–83, 107–108
countercultures, 74–76
counterrevolutionary movements, 201
cover letters, 203
crime. *see also* deviance and social control
 prison population and, 189–190
 types of, 187–189
critical gerontology approach, 97
cross-linkage theory, 93
cross-sectional surveys, 56
crowds, 200
crude birth rate, 170
culture, 69–78
 cultural beliefs, 73–74
 cultural capital, 76
 cultural relativism, 75–76
 cultural symbols, 74
 cultural symbols and social identity, 83
 cultural transmission theory, 156
 cultural values, 72
 culture of poverty, 125–126
 culture shock, 70
 defined, 70
 generally, 70–74
 subcultures and countercultures, 74–76
cumulative disadvantage, 158

D

Darwin, Charles, 134
Davis, Kingsley, 126
definition of the situation, 84
demography
 defined, 168–169
 demographic transition theory, 174
 fertility and, 169–170
 mortality and, 170–171
dependent variables, 55

deviance and social control, 183–195
 alcohol use among college students, 186
 context of deviance, 185–186
 deviance, defined, 184–185
 explaining deviance and crime, 190–192
 functions and dysfunctions of deviance, 193
 social control, defined, 186–187
 social control and crime, 187–189
 social control and prison population, 189–190
differential association theory, 191
discrimination
 defined, 145–146
 environmental racism/discrimination, 179
disengagement theory, 94
Division of Labor in Society, The (Durkheim), 26–27
dogs, culture and, 71
domestic servants, migration and, 172–173
Domhoff, G. William, 123
dramaturgical approach, 84
dual labor market theory, 172–173
DuBois, W. E. B., 31
Durkheim, Emile, 13–14, 26–28, 41, 106
dysfunction, 42
dysfunctions of deviance, 193

E

earnings gap, between men and women, 157, 158–161
ecological footprint, 176–177
ecology, 176
economic base, 24–26
education, social conflict perspective, 43–44

homeownership
    racial and ethnic inequality, 144
    wealth distribution and, 122–123
horizontal mobility, 128–129
Hull House, 30–31
hypothesis, 54

I

"I, The," 83–84
Ibn Khaldun, 22
impression management, 85
income
    defined, 122
    gender inequality and earning gap, 157,
        158–161
independent variables, 55
index crime, 188
India, population of, 168
Industrial Revolution, 22–23
inequality of condition, 120–121
inequality of opportunity, 120–121
informal social control, 187
in-groups, 109
institutional review boards (IRB), 64
intergenerational mobility, 129
International Association of Athletics
        Federations, 154
international migration, 171
interpretative sociology, 28–29
intersectionality, 158
intersex individuals, 152
interviews, 59–60
intragenerational mobility, 129

J

Jablonski, Nina, 136–137
job skills. *see* workplace
Johnson, Lyndon, 124

K

Kanter, Rosabeth Moss, 121
Kyoto Protocol, 177

L

labeling theory, 191–192
Lady Gaga, 184
language, nonmaterial culture and, 71–72
latent functions, 41–42
Latinos. *see also* racial and ethnic inequality
        immigrant population in U.S., 140
        skin color and, 138
law, 187–189
law of hypodescent, 135
Law of Three Stages, 24
life course perspective, 97
life expectancy, 170
literature review, 53
longevity, 170
longitudinal surveys, 56
looking-glass self, 81–83

M

macrosociology, 53
macro theories of aging, 96
Malthus, Thomas Robert, 173–174
manifest function, 41–42
Marger, Martin, 121
Marx, Karl, 24–26, 29, 43–45
mass hysteria, 200
master status, 112–113
material culture, 70–71
matrix of domination, 158
"Me, The," 83–84
Mead, George Herbert, 45, 83–84
means of production, 25

prefrontal cortex, 7
prejudice, 145–146
presentation of self, 85
preventive checks, 173–174
primary groups, 107–109
proletariat, 25
Protestant Ethic and the Spirit of Capitalism, The (Weber), 29
psychological perspective, 6, 8–10
public issues, 16–18

Q

quantitative and qualitative methods, 51–66
    qualitative methods, defined, 54
    quantitative methods, defined, 54
    research ethics, 64
    scientific method, 52–62
    triangulation, 62–63

R

race. *see also* racial and ethnic inequality
    biology, and social thinking, 134–136
    cultural beliefs about, 73–74
    defined, 134
    skin color and social thinking, 136–137
    social conflict perspective and, 45
    as social construction, 137–138
    social stratification and poverty, 125
racial and ethnic inequality, 133–148
    defined, 141–144
    ethnicity, defined, 134
    race, biology, and social thinking, 134–136
    race, defined, 134
    race, skin color, and social thinking, 136–137
    race as social construction, 137–138
    racial formations, 138–146
    U.S. prison population, 189–190
racism, 38–39, 145–146
reference groups, 109–110
reformist movements, 201
regressive movements, 201
religion
    Durkheim on suicide and, 13–14
    two-sex category system and, 153–154
    Weber on economy and, 29
research ethics, 64
research methods. *see* quantitative and qualitative methods
resocialization, 86
resource mobilization theory, 202
resumes, 203
revolutionary movements, 201
role conflict, 113–114
role strain, 113–114

S

Sanders, Clinton, 71
sandwich generation, 99
scientific method
    data analysis, qualitative methods, 61–62
    data analysis, quantitative methods, 57
    data collection, qualitative methods, 57–61
    data collection, quantitative method, 54–57
    data collection and deciding method, 53–54
    defined, 4–5, 52
    finding topics, 52–53
secondary groups, 107–109
Semenya, Caster, 154
semistructured interviews, 59

Servicemen's Readjustment Act of 1944
    (G.I. Bill), 198
sex. *see also* gender
    defined, 151
    sex category system, 153–156
sexism, 161. *see also* gender
sexual harassment, 160, 161
simple random sampling, 57
skin color, racial inequality and, 136–137
Smith, Adam, 26
social change, 197–200
social conflict perspective, 43–45
social construct, 53
social constructionism, 96
social construction of reality, 46
social control. *see also* deviance and social
        control
    defined, 186–187
    law and crime, 187–189
    prison population and, 189–190
social groups, 105–119
    defined, 105–107
    formal organizations and bureaucracies,
        110–112
    in-groups and out-groups, 109
    master status and status inconsistency,
        112–113
    primary and secondary groups, 107–
        109
    reference groups, 109–110
    role conflict and role strain, 113–114
    social institutions, 115
social inequality, 120–121
socialization, 79–88
    agents of socialization, 85–86
    defined, 80
    development of social self, 81–85
    gender socialization, 159
    nature *versus* nurture, 80–81
    process of, 80

"social maze," defined, 12
social mobility, 128–129
social movements
    defined, 201
    social movement theory, 202
social roles
    defined, 111–112
    social roles and aging, 92
social self, development of, 81–85
social status, 111–112
social stratification, 119–131
    defined, 120
    party, status, and class, 121–123
    poverty and, 124–127
    social inequality and, 120–121
    social mobility, 128–129
social structure, 111–112
social theory, 37–49
    social conflict perspective, 43–45
    sociological theory, 37–40
    structural functionalist perspective,
        41–42
    symbolic interactionist perspective,
        45–47
society
    defined, 11
    social change, 197–200
    social conflict perspective, 44–46
    socioeconomic gap between Whites
        and Blacks, 144–146
    structural functionalist perspective and,
        41–42
socioeconomic status (SES). *see also* social
        stratification
    defined, 128
    racial inequality and, 144–146
sociological imagination, 16–18
sociological perspective, 3–20
    biological perspective compared to, 6–8
    defined, 11–16

CPSIA information can be obtained
at www.ICGtesting.com
Printed in the USA
LVHW011610191218
600569LV00003B/7/P

9 781465 238368